MUSLIM BROTHERHOOD: THE THREAT IN OUR BACKYARD

Cathy Hinners

ISBN: 1530500176
ISBN 13: 9781530500178

DEDICATION

In the last few years, my life has been different. Countless hours are spent on the computer, on the phone and travelling. I don't like what I do, but it's what I am *supposed* to do. Through all of this, my husband Tom has been by my side, supporting my work and always so proud, and for that I am so thankful. I love you! My sister Carol has always been my best friend, my best shoulder, and my best listener. I know you worry about me, but I also know how proud of me you are, and I love you for being you. I thank my brothers Keith and Kevin for unknowingly making me strong, stubborn, and like I could conquer anything. I Love you both. I have been inspired and guided by so many, Victor and Bill, your advice has always grounded me and made me think. My friends Geraldine, Rhonda and Irene, your support is endless no matter how time goes by without talking. You are the best. Joanne, Joan, Daniel, Andy and Vince, you welcomed me with open arms, and have opened so many doors through which I have met some incredible people. Being your friend and colleague has meant a great deal. Michael, being your "top cop" has also opened doors I never thought possible, and I look forward to future ventures. Dan you have also given me opportunities for my voice to be heard in so many places.

To my pets Casey, Champ, Zoey and Max, you keep my feet warm, my lap filled, and my spirits high. A pet's love is unconditional, and through all the madness, you each make me smile.

My angels, Mom, Dad and Aunt Mary, keep watch over us in these tough times. We will meet again someday.

Finally,

To Ken, who took a chance I would follow through, thank you for starting me on this journey that has allowed me to open the eyes of thousands of my fellow officers across the country. From our meetings in PA with Pete, the laughs we had as we grew tired of planning, to the countless hours you spent putting it all together, I am thankful and grateful for the opportunity. I am forever the princess.

PREFACE

Like so many of you, the first time I heard about terrorism, was the day airplanes flew into buildings killing thousands of innocent Americans. Since 9/11, our lives have been changed, whether you know it or not. Life before that day was simple, or so it seemed. It is the unknown, that has been occurring for decades we should fear now. The infiltration of a once silent enemy, has morphed into an empowered and emboldened one. It is called the Muslim Brotherhood. They, like the enemy that brought us to our knees on 9/11 have the same ideology, and the same agenda, just a different means of carrying it out. This isn't about hate, bigotry or racism, it is about preserving and protecting our future. We must define and identify those that wish to do us harm, dismantle America and our foundation. My hope is that if just one bit of information from this book opens your eyes, it is one more voice to spread the word. We can beat this enemy, as long as you know who is in your own backyard.

INTRODUCTION

A s a police officer, attending **daily roll call** was the first duty prior to patrol. It was during that time details of important incidents and events were shared for officer safety and awareness. This book was written with hopes you also will gain insight and awareness of the subject of the Muslim Brotherhood in our own backyard. Each chapter is taken from articles from my website, dailyrollcall.com which is unlike any other book, as each article contains words from their own documents, and open social media.

For years I have followed the workings of the Muslim brotherhood in America, but it has never been this personal. The Muslim Brotherhood is no longer an organization that quietly lingers in the background, they have become emboldened and empowered by sympathizers and supporters.

The Muslim Brotherhood is alive and well in the United States of America. Why is that important? Because the Muslim Brotherhood, also known as the Ikhwan, came to America with the explicit agenda of establishing a caliphate, one law, (Sharia) one government and one God (Allah).

To help set guidelines and goals for Islamists living in America, Muslim Brotherhood members wrote a detailed document called "An Explanatory Memorandum On the General Strategic Goal for the Group in North America".

This document is a detailed account of how and who will be utilized to implement these goals, and the organizations needed to be formed. The relationship of the Muslim Brotherhood with the government of the United States started in the 1950's, and has grown since. The current expediency of its growth and the depth of infiltration should be a great concern for all Americans. Members and supporters of the Muslim Brotherhood have infiltrated not only our government on all levels, but our military, law enforcement, schools and religious institutions.

"The opportunity to secure ourselves against defeat lies
in our own hands,
but the opportunity of defeating the enemy is provided by
the enemy himself".

Sun Tzu

MEET THE AUTHOR

Cathy Hinners is a decorated, re-tired police officer from the Albany N.Y Police Dept. Upon her retire-ment, she developed and instructed a 3-day class for law enforcement titled Middle Eastern: Crime, Culture and Community, based on the knowledge she acquired while working in an emerging Middle Eastern/Muslim area.

Cathy also worked as a sub-con-tract instructor for the U.S Department of Homeland Security's Center for Domestic Preparedness, where she delivered mobile training to members of the New York Police Department, the National Guard, and various other law enforcement agencies. A segment of the class Cathy instructed was on Weapons of Mass Destruction (WMD) and bomb recognition.

In an on-going effort to learn and be effective in her training, Cathy completed several U.S Department of Homeland Security courses in areas such as explosives at New Mexico Tech, Threat and Vulnerability Assessments at West Point Military Academy, and Technical Emergency Response Training for CBRNE Incidents at the Center for Domestic Preparedness in Anniston AL.

Several other certifications were also received through courses with the New York State Department of Homeland Security, such as Domestic Terrorist incidents, the Incident Command System (all levels) and Active Shooter Response.

Upon her retirement and move to Tennessee, Cathy became active in investigating and exposing the Muslim Brotherhood organizations and individuals within Tennessee, and in America. Cathy now travels throughout the states speaking on the incursion of terrorist organizations infiltrating as well as the threats in your own backyard.

In June of 2015, the Southern Poverty Law Center named Cathy one of the 12 most "hard-lined, anti- Muslim" women in America along with Laura Ingraham, Anne Coulter, Bridgette Gabriel and Clare Lopez.

https://www.splcenter.org/fighting-hate/intelligence-report/2015/women-against-islam

Cathy is the founder of Dailyrollcall.com, where she exposes issues pertaining to Islam. Dailyrollcall is also a group of retired law enforcement and military personnel that actively investigate and vet tips given by concerned citizens.

Cathy is a regular guest on Nashville's Super Talk 99.7 radio, every Monday. Other radio segments done on a regular basis are with Red State Radio's Scott Adams Show, and the Melody Burns show.

Articles written by Cathy can be found on her website, www.dailyrollcall.com and on www.familysecuritymatters.org.

TABLE OF CONTENTS

WHY THE ISLAMIZATION OF AMERICA IS BEGINNING?

Do not believe for one second ISIS wants America to "hate Muslims". That is the latest in a string of narratives put forth by the Muslim communities across America. By supporting the decision to halt Syrian refugees, we have somehow become proxy sympathizers to the ISIS cause, playing into their hands by our supposed hatred of Muslims. That hatred then drives young Muslims to join Islamic terror groups, which Muslims claim, are killing more Muslims than any other group.

The truth is, by stopping Syrians who have vowed to enter Europe and the United States under the guise of refugees, their mission has been disrupted. In order for the Islamic caliphate to be reestablished, the population of Muslims must be great in numbers. What better way to reach this goal, then to continually flood our nation with Muslims? It is Islamic history in the making.

To understand how history is repeating itself, one must understand it to begin with. Muslims believe there is only one God, Allah, who through the Prophet Muhammad revealed the words of the Qur'an. The traditions and sayings of the prophet are contained in the Sunnah and the Hadiths. This making the trilogy of books most important to Muslims. In order for a Muslim to be "good", they must imitate his life, as prescribed by those books.

In summary, the early years of Mohammed, described as his years in Mecca, he was peaceful and while he desired to convert others to Islam, he accepted those that practiced their own religion, which led to a very small number of Muslims. On his hijra to Yathrib (Medina), Muhammad rejected the offer of peaceful co-existence. His religion was obviously intended to dominate others, not to be equal. It was in Medina that Islam became a political and military ideology. Before his death, non-believers (infidels) were evicted or enslaved, and converted under the threat of death if they did not.

Put into context, this is what is occurring throughout the world today. Here in America, Muslims have been performing Dawa, (spreading the word of Islam) in the hopes of bringing all people to it. Dawa is a religious obligation that every "good" Muslim must perform. This is why interfaith forums are so important, as are doing good deeds within their communities. Making non-believers see the goodness and oneness of their religion. In addition to Dawa, Muslims must strive to live by Islamic law, not man made law, which Muhammad rejected.

Today, ISIS is showing the world the return of their caliphate (an Islamic state) commanded by the Prophet. Non-Muslims are being slaughtered if conversion is rejected, and Sharia (Islamic Law) is not adhered to. As their numbers grow, they conquer more land. It is happening in Europe, and is now happening in America.

HOW THE ISLAMIZATION OF AMERICA IS OCCURRING?

M uslims intent on bringing about the revival of the global caliphate have no issue with articulating how it will be done. For years, the Ikhwan (Muslim Brotherhood) has carefully executed the plan laid out in its manifesto, "An Explanatory Memorandum On the General Strategic Goal for the Group in North America". This document was submitted as evidence by the prosecution in the 2008 Holy Land Foundation trial, in Dallas TX, where 109 indictments were handed down against several members of Hamas and the Muslim Brotherhood. This trial was the largest terrorism funding case in America to date. From the manifesto:

Understanding the role of the Muslim Brother in North America:

"The process of settlement is a "Civilization-Jihadist Process" with all the word means. The Ikhwan must understand that their work in America is a kind of grand Jihad in eliminating and destroying the Western civilization from within and "sabotaging" its miserable house by their hands and the hands of the believers so that it is eliminated and God's religion is made victorious over all other

religions. Without this level of understanding, we are not up to this challenge and have not prepared ourselves for Jihad yet. It is a Muslim's destiny to perform Jihad and work wherever he is and wherever he lands until the final hour comes, and there is no escape from that destiny except for those who chose to slack"

(See the entire Explanatory Memorandum on The Strategic Goal for the Group in North America at the end of this book)

The Methodology of Dawa is another lengthy, but informative tool we must read to gain insight on how Muslims use Dawa (the proselytizing of Islam) not only to exploit the caring nature of Christians and Americans, but cause division among them. Written by Shamim Siddiqui, it reveals the deceitful ways Muslims use their faith to garner trust and support within their non-Muslim communities.

(the Methodology of Dawa can be found under documents on Dailyrollcall.com)

The following are excerpts from this book, which help to shed light on their true intentions.

" When the struggle between Haq (truth) and Batil (falsehoods) acquires momentum and the tension increases along with it, the common folk will start taking sides with either of the two groups. In due course of time, the society will stand divided in two definite camps, one the supporters of Haq and the other the henchmen of vested interests. The struggle will thus continue, sometimes slowly and sometimes at an accelerated pace. The polarization on the basis of support to the Islamic ideology will go on mounting in its wake. It will be visible in every walk of life." (Chapter IV Page 42)'

"The Muslims of America may concentrate their numerical strength, through migration to that state, and try to make it a model Islamic society within the power available under the constitution of the U.S.A. and what it does not prohibit."

" This will pave the way to get hold of other states in a like manner. Thus, without disturbing or violating the constitution of the U.S.A., they can prepare the ground for the emergence of Islam as a way of life acceptable to the electorate of this country. This will also prepare the way, in due course of time, to send their representatives to Congress and the Senate. There they will be able to create a strong lobby in Washington for the promotion of Islam and its cause in this country as well as elsewhere in the world" (Chapter IV Page 45)

" To me, it appears as the fate of the American people. They are in need of some ideology. It is we the Muslims who are here by Allah's will to provide that opportunity to this great nation which is humiliated everywhere due to lack of a superb ideology of its own. It matters little for the Islamic Movement as to whether it takes one or many decades to make the ideology of Islam prevail over the mental horizon of the American people. The action must be taken now. The Movement must be set out forthwith. The struggle for making Allah's Deen dominant must take shape without any further lapse of time" (Chapter IV page 46)

As American parents struggle to stop the infiltration of Islam in a religious context in our public school textbooks, Islamic schools are promoting something else. Ridiculing Christians and Jews. One textbook, used in Islamic schools in Knoxville and Nashville TN is "What Islam is all about" by Yahiya Emerick.

In a lesson on "friends" (page 366), there are five conditions that are attached to having non-Muslim friends. Using Sura 4:140 and 6:68 as examples, it states:

"You have already been given the command in the book, that when you hear the signs of Allah being insulted or joked with, you are not to sit with them unless they start talking about something else. If you stayed with them while they were insulting Allah, then you would be like them. Allah will gather all hypocrites and unbelievers in hell".

5

These passages, taken from their own documents and books are supplemental to the Hadiths and Sunnah, which further pre-scribes the actions "*good*" Muslims must follow. Through legal means, (and other ways) their playbook has been revealed. They do not deny or dispute the contents. Only those that are blind or in denial do.

The Muslim Brotherhood/Hamas Motto:
Allah is our objective
the Prophet is our leader
the Quran is our law
Jihad is our way
and dying in the way of Allah is our highest hope.

ISLAMIC ORGANIZATIONS IN OUR OWN BACKYARD

"If ignorant both of your enemy and yourself, you are certain to be in peril".

Sun Tzu

Islam is not a religion, but a complete way of life. It is political, it is militarized, it is our adversary and our downfall. Now that you know why and how America is being Islamized, identifying the organizations is imperative. The following groups fall under the umbrella of the Muslim Brotherhood, and are active nationally. While there are 29 listed in the manifesto, below are ones most recognized and progressive.

The Islamic Society of North America– (ISNA) Headquarters located in Plainfield IN, seeks to spread Sharia law globally and in the U.S.A. Holding several conventions a year, they are known for radical speakers, which often promote the concept of Jihad.

The North American Islamic Trust– (NAIT) is a subsidiary of the Islamic Society of North America, it's a U.S.-based Islamic trust that holds the titles of hundreds of Islamic properties and mosques and has close ties to the Muslim Brotherhood.

The International Institute for Islamic Thought– Inventor of the word Islamophobia, (IIIT) this is an Islamic institution with ties to the extremist Saudi-Wahhabi movement. Muslim convert Susan Douglass, who worked for the Council on Islamic Education (CIE) has authored lesson plans, advisories, guidelines and pamphlets to promote Islam in public schools, and has had several books published under this organization.

The Muslim Student Association- is recognized as student religious organizations on over 600 college campuses throughout the United States. Their purpose is to spread the word of Islam (dawa) to students, faculty and community. They are responsible for bringing radical speakers to campuses, as well as involvement with the Black Lives Matter movement and the Students for Justice in Palestine. Each chapter has a different logo, but falls under the national MSA.

The United States Council of Muslim Organizations (USCMO) – The first political party formed by the Muslim Brotherhood in 2014. Their Inaugural Dinner was attended and supported by U.S Congressman Keith Ellison (MN) and Congressman Andre Carson (IN). The founding members of the USCMO are the original Muslim Brotherhood organizations operating within the United States.

The Council on American Islamic Relations (CAIR) formerly the Islamic Association of Palestine- claims to be the largest Muslim grassroots group in America. Is an un-indicted co-conspirator in our nation's largest terrorism funding trial, The Holy Land Foundation, for monetarily supporting Hamas. Its Executive Director of the National chapter, Nihad Awad, is a self-proclaimed supporter of Hamas. CAIR is a designated Terrorist organization in the United Arab Emirates (U.A.E). CAIR has submitted arguments to a Texas District Court to have the label un-indicted co-conspirator removed, however the judge ruled there was substantial evidence to prove they did in fact fund Hamas.

CAIR has chapters in several states, and is famous for its lawsuits and demands for sensitivity training. CAIR has members in law enforcement, city councils, and federal agencies with several members serving in the White House.

Other Islamic organizations located in your area should be identified and watched for hosting interfaith forums, opposition to proposed legislation, lobbying, immigration and refugee involvement, and educational involvement with public schools. While they may not be exactly the same names, this is a start of what to look for.

American Muslim Advisory Councils (AMAC) – Law Enforcement training
American Center for Outreach – Lobbying
Islamic Network Group – Education
Faith and Culture Center – Interfaith
Muslim Women's Council – Interfaith, and Community Service
Connecting Cultures – Sensitivity training, and education
Council on Islamic Education- Education and textbooks
Institute of Religion and Civic Values- Education

Islamophile Organizations

Family of Abraham
Tennessee Immigrant and Refugee Rights Coalition (TIRRC)
Catholic Charities
Church World Service (CWS)
Ethiopian Community Development Council (ECDC)
Episcopal Migration Ministries (EMM)

Hebrew Immigrant Aid Society (HIAS)
International Rescue Committee (IRC)
US Committee for Refugees and Immigrants (USCRI)
Lutheran Immigration and Refugee Services (LIRS)
United States Conference of Catholic Bishops (USCCB)
World Relief Corporation (WR)
And so many more...

THE TERRORISTS IN YOUR BACKYARD...

It's time to wake up America. Hamas, the Muslim Brotherhood, Jamaat Ul Fuqra, Al Shabaab, Hizb Ut Tahir, Al Qaida, the Taliban and more, have a presence within our borders and unfortunately all use the guise of religion for the protection of the First Amendment.

So who and where are they?

Hamas/CAIR (Council On American Islamic Relations, formerly known as the Islamic Association for Palestine) has at least 29 chapters in the United States. Hamas headquarters was in Chicago IL.

Muslim Brotherhood: the majority of mosques and Islamic Centers are operated by ISNA (Islamic Society of North America) and funded by NAIT (North American Islamic Trust) including The Islamic Center of Nashville, Islamic Center of Murfreesboro and the Islamic Center of Tampa FL. Groups such as the ACO (American Center for Outreach) and AMAC (American Muslim Advisory Council) both located in Tennessee and Illinois, are run by Muslim Brotherhood supporters.

Jamaat Ul Fuqra aka MOA (Muslims of America) is a Pakistani organization present is Dover TN, called Islamville. There are 36 of these communities nationwide, including its headquarters in Hancock NY (which we have visited on 3 occasions) York SC, GA and TX are also home to these communities. Jamaat Ul Fuqra was responsible for the beheading of Wall Street reporter Daniel Pearl as he was being led to the founder of the group, Sheik Mubarak Ali Gilani.

Al-Shabaab: With the largest population in Minneapolis MN, they are currently known to be recruiting in other states prison population. In 2008, Minnesota had the first American suicide bomber, Shirwa Ahmed who left MN with 4 other young men to join the fight in Somali. This story is worth a read! (http://gate-sofvienna.net/2014/02/the-al-shabaab-connection/)

Hizb Ut Tahrir: Their headquartered in Chicago Il, and their goal is the return of the global caliphate, or Islamic State. (http://english.hizbuttahrir.org/)

Al Qaida: Bowling Green KY, was found to be the home of Iraqi "refugees" that were later found to be Al Qaida operatives that had been brought to the U.S by the Refugee Resettlement program.

Taliban: With the story of the treasonous Army soldier Bowe Bergdahl all but out of the media, the Taliban trained soldier is now free to roam the base in TX. Being held by the Taliban for several years, the intelligence world believes he may be a threat at some time in the future. Lest we forget John Walker Lind, the American Taliban, surely there are more we have yet to find.

So what can you do? Expose the organizations and individuals that support any of these terrorist organizations. Boycott their businesses, protest their existence in the United States. Why are they allowed to function in the United States? Educate. Learn about who and where they are and spread the word.

Do you know who's in your backyard?

ARE AMERICANS WILLING TO SUBMIT TO ISLAM? YOU ALREADY ARE... PART 1

We Americans are on the path to our own demise.

The free world was jolted off of theirs, first on January 7 2015, with the massacre of journalists in Paris France, then again on November 15, 2015 where 139 people were slaughtered as they attended various recreational activities. What will it take for us to take back the reigns of our own destiny? We are at war. If our own government won't identify the enemy, it is time for Americans to do so and call it what it is... Islam. Islam means submission, are Americans willing to submit without a fight?

The four stages of Islamic conquest* clearly defines the enemy and its goal for each phase. Unfortunately, America has already succumbed to two. Keep in mind, nearly every conflict in the world involves Islam threatening native populations.

STAGE 1: INFILTRATION
Muslims are moving to non-Muslim countries in increasing numbers and the beginning of cultural conflicts are visible, but often subtle.

The first migration wave to non-Muslim "host" country. This occurred as early as 1947, when Muslim Brotherhood member Sayid Qutb studied in the U.S then returned to Egypt where he wrote extensively on his disdain for American culture. By 1963, the Muslim Brotherhood established what is now the Muslim Student Association. With the success of the MSA, other Muslim Brotherhood groups began to form and take root. Sayid Qutb is the author of "Milestones".

The appeal for humanitarian tolerance from the host society. Being that so many Middle Easterners were arriving in the U.S from violent regions, here they found safe refuge, hence the victim status was given to many. Today they still embrace victim-hood.

Attempts to portray Islam as peaceful and Muslims as victims of misunderstanding and racism (even though Islam is not a 'race'). History clearly shows Islam and its Prophet to be violent. In the Koran, there are two periods through which Muhammad went through. The one which Muslims always refer to is the brief time Muhammad was peaceful, which ended when he failed to convert others in large numbers. He then resorted to violence and became political, and remained that way until his death. His actions and words are articulated in the Sunnah and Hadiths, which he commands "good" Muslims to obey. Good Muslims must follow his example, which were ultimately violent.

High Muslim birth rate in host country increase Muslim population. The only way to ensure the world can return to a pure form, is to establish the caliphate where Islam and its law (Sharia) are superior, therefore there must be a majority of Muslims which can only occur with high birth rates. (Somalis may have 4-8 children).

Mosques used to spread Islam and dislike of host country and culture. Mosques, and now Islamic Centers, are no longer just for "prayer", but rather community centers, providing services for the Muslim community. However, historically mosques were used for military operations, and were where Muhammad issued his fatwas (legal rulings) Mosques were and are still the center for radicalization. (i.e. The Islamic Center of Nashville TN was the center of radicalization for Carlos Bledsoe, aka Abdulhakim Mujahid Muhammad. There he received training by the Imam of the same name, and later shot and killed Army recruiter Sgt. Andy Long in Arkansas, all in the name of Islam.

http://www.cnn.com/2009/CRIME/06/01/arkansas.recruiter. shooting/

Calls to criminalize "Islamophobia" as a hate crime. The rise of people across the world disagreeing and refusing to submit to the demands of Muslims has led to Islamists (particularly in the U.S where we have freedom of speech) to coin a phrase "Islamophobia" in hopes of instilling fear in those that speak the truth about Islam. (after all, no one wants to be labeled or called a name!) However, here in America, it is being taken quite seriously, with the current administration, including the Dept. of Justice, actually considering a U.N Resolution (16/18) called the Defamation of Religion Law. Former Sect. of State, Hillary Clinton was part of a series of meetings with the OIC (Organization of Islamic Cooperation)

http://oicun.org/ which has drafted laws pertaining to the criminalization of speaking out against religions, but particularly Islam. Very dangerous!

Threatened legal action for perceived discrimination. Currently an organization called CAIR (Council on American Islamic Relations) which was co-founded and is led by Hamas supporter Nihad Awad, is leading the charge for jihad law-fare. Repeatedly and continuously filing frivolous law suits against anyone (businesses, schools, law enforcement, the military, and individuals) is causing the backlog and disruption of our legal and civil law system. This all done in the hopes those institutions or individuals will eventually give in and allow whatever demands the Muslims are making. Being that is also becomes a financial drain to fight these lawsuits, the demands are met even sooner. Currently CAIR is suing the United States Navy, for not allowing a Muslim to wear his beard. http://dailycaller.com/2014/12/29/cair-sues-u-s-navy-over-right-to-have-a-beard-if-you-are-a-muslim/

To read more ludicrous, ridiculous suits, go to http://www.cair.com

Offers of "interfaith dialogue" to indoctrinate non-Muslims. The goal of every "good Muslim" is to convert non-Muslims or kafirs (non- believer or infidel) to Islam. Interfaith forums have become the most popular way for Islamists to perform Dawa, which is an obligation under their doctrine. Typically, these forums will feature of panel of leaders from different faiths (but always will include a Christian and a Jew) where they will each deliver the message of commonality. However, anyone that knows the Koran, knows of it violence, and questions the statement from the co-founder of CAIR, "Islam isn't in America to be equal to any other faith, but to become dominant. The Koran, the Muslim book of scripture, should be the highest authority in America, and Islam the only accepted religion on Earth." is not allowed to be a panelist. Questions regarding any of the Korans contradictions are always met with elusive, often scrambled answers. Over a year ago, the Islamic Center of Murfreesboro TN hosted a forum called" God's Books" which oddly enough featured a renowned, self -described, documented member of the Muslim Brotherhood, Jamal Badawi.

For more on exactly how Dawa and interfaith forums are scams read The Methodology of Dawa by Shamm Siddiqui.

Stage one laid a foundation for which the Muslims tested our Constitution, our laws, and us as a people. The mere fact we have arrived in Stage 2 means we are failing

ARE AMERICANS WILLING TO SUBMIT TO ISLAM? YOU ALREADY ARE...PART 2

U nfortunately Stage two brings with it the suppression of a number of our Constitutional rights, our culture and our own religious beliefs. Please read that sentence again. Islamists across the board have been saying America is no longer a melting pot, but rather a mosaic. Refusing to assimilate, and insisting to be different eventually causes division and radicalization. While some occurrences below may have subtle or seemingly insignificant examples, you will see stage two is clearly in action.

STAGE 2 CONSOLIDATION OF POWER
Muslim immigrants and host country converts continue demands for accommodation in employment, education, social services and courts.

Proselytizing increases; Establishment and Recruitment of Jihadi cells. With Dawa (the proselytizing of Islam) being ramped up as stages progress, it comes along with the mindset of radicals that if conversion doesn't occur on its own, if people of other faiths don't see Islam as being the only true religion, Jihad will be the only resource left. Jihad is in fact, an unspoken pillar to which every good Muslim must obey.

Efforts to convert alienated segments of the population to Islam. Unfortunately segments of our population that have succumbed to being homeless, those on welfare, homosexuals, prisoners, and generally those that are misguided with no direction, or that may be disgruntled or feel abandoned have become prime targets for Islamists. Muslim communities have taken food to the homeless, opened weekend medical clinics, marched with gays, and brought hope to those in prison. All gestures of good will and humanity, however it is always for an ulterior motive. Who will be remembered as helping those in need? The Muslims. Who foolishly bites the hand that feeds them? Therefore, they have gained sympathy and gained people who will undoubtedly stand up against those that speak out on Islam. But that is one side of Islam's face, here is how they feel about homosexuality, you know one of the groups they embrace. "This point is important because one of the main aims of sex is to produce children in order to continue human life. Homosexuality does not yield any children. It is a relationship purely for the sake of pleasure, which is not only unnatural, but leads to disease and death".

Read entire article here: http://www.soundvision.com/info/education/sex/kidstips.asp

Revisionist efforts to Islamize history. Islamists are now claiming Muslims founded America not Columbus. See here http://www.wnd.com/2014/11/nato-allys-president-muslims-discovered-america/

Efforts to destroy historic evidence that reveal true Islamism.

Increased anti-western propaganda and psychological warfare. After the horrific terrorist attacks by Islamists in Paris, Muslims across the country attempted to blame America by insisting the attacks were the result of the released Abu Gharib torture report and pictures. America is consistently seen as the great oppressor to even those that choose to live here.

Efforts to recruit allies who share similar goals (communists, anarchists). Muslims for Ferguson. https://www.facebook.com/Muslims4Ferguson

Attempts to indoctrinate children to the Islamist viewpoint. The discovery of Pro Islam, anti-Christian (or nothing at all on Christianity) rhetoric in a vast number of textbooks throughout the country, as well as cartoons, dolls, and toys is evidence of the quest to plant a seed in the minds of children. Back in 2008, a doll from Fisher Price called the Coo and Cuddle Doll was released without anyone knowing the doll said "Islam is the Light" amongst her cooing. The Nintendo DS Baby Pals game also says the same thing. (I personally have 2 of the dolls and one of the Nintendo games)

In addition to toys, the rise in field trips to mosques and the demand for female students to dress in a particular way is very disturbing.

http://eagnews.org/colorado-school-district-requires-girls-to-cover-ankles-wear-head-scarves-for-trip-to-mosque/

Increased efforts to intimidate, silence and eliminate non-- Muslims.

Efforts to introduce blasphemy and hate laws in order to silence critics

Use of charities to recruit supporters and fund jihad. The 5th pillar of Islam, Zakat, has been celebrated by terrorists such as Osama Bin Laden as the perfect way to fund jihad. "Your duty is to support the Mujahedeen with money and men. I have experienced Jihad myself and I know how costly it can be. The Zakat of one affluent Muslim merchant is enough to finance all the Jihadi front against our enemies", and Yusef al Qaradawi who stated: "Collecting money for the Mujahedeen was not a donation or a gift but a duty necessitated by the sacrifices they made for the Muslim nation" Groups such as Islamic Relief USA and the Syrian Sunrise Foundation, are just 2 of the organizations that have openly funded jihad.

https://syriansunrisefoundation.org/

Covert efforts to bring about the destruction of host society from within. In the words of the Muslim Brotherhood: Understanding the role of the Muslim Brother in North America:

> *"The process of settlement is a "Civilization-Jihadist Process" with all the word means. The Ikhwan must understand that their work in America is a kind of grand Jihad in eliminating and destroying the Western civilization from within and "sabotaging" its miserable house by their hands and the hands of the believers so that it is eliminated and God's religion is made victorious over all other religions"*

Development of Muslim political base in non-Muslim host society. Recently formed, the U.S Council of Muslim Organizations (USCMO) currently consists of 8 Muslim groups that believe by 2016 they will have the ability and power to sway an election. Note: all 8 groups are Muslim Brotherhood, and according to their own plan called "An Explanatory Memorandum on the General Strategic Goal for the Group in North America" this is a must to obtain their agenda

Islamic Financial networks fund political growth, acquisition of land.

Highly visible assassination of critics aimed to intimidate opposition. NA

Tolerance of non-Muslims diminishes. NA

Greater demands to adopt strict Islamic conduct• Clandestine amassing of weapons and explosives in hidden locations.

Overt disregard/rejection of non-Muslim society's legal system, culture.

Efforts to undermine and destroy power base of non-Muslim religions including and especially Jews and Christians. NA

Although Stage Two is not completely fulfilled, you can see it has most certainly been set in motion. Elements of Stage 3 have just begun, as the larger the population grows, the more empowered and emboldened the Islamists become.

ARE AMERICANS WILLING TO SUBMIT TO ISLAM? YOU ALREADY ARE... PART 3

I f America continues on its current path, the next few years will be unlike any we've experienced in our history. As we watch other countries fall to their knees, we must listen to what they are telling us. If we don't, we will continue to be victims by our own hands. Although Stage 2 has not yet been completed, there are factors in Stage 3 we can say have occurred or are currently. If NA is written after each point, it has not occurred to our knowledge. This is based on actions within the U.S

STAGE 3: OPEN WAR on LEADERSHIP & CULTURE
Open violence to impose Sharia law and associated cultural restrictions; NA

Rejection of host government, subjugation of other religions and customs. NA

Intentional efforts to undermine the host government & culture.

Acts of barbarity to intimidate citizens and foster fear and submission While acts of barbarity have certainly occurred, it is troubling to say America has failed to fully recognize their significance. The beheading of a woman in OK was certainly not workplace violence, but certainly was a Muslim following the words of their holy book, the Koran. In Sura 47 verse 4, it states: "So when you meet those who disbelieve [in battle], strike [their] necks until, when you have inflicted slaughter upon them, then secure their bonds, and either [confer] favor afterwards or ransom [them] until the war lays down its burdens. That [is the command]. And if Allah had willed, He could have taken vengeance upon them [Himself], but [He ordered armed struggle] to test some of you by means of others. And those who are killed in the cause of Allah – never will He waste their deeds"

Yes, they do believe they are at battle, as the goal is to reestablish the caliphate at all costs.

All opposition is challenged and either eradicated or silenced. Even as this is being written, Islamists across America are beginning to make the case that free speech is a good thing except when they don't like what is being said. (http://radio.foxnews. com/toddstarnes/top-stories/american-muslims-want-limits-on-free-speech.html)

Mass execution of non-Muslims. NA

Widespread ethnic cleansing by Islamic militias. NA

Rejection and defiance of host society secular laws or culture. Christmas traditions have all but been eliminated in public venues, the pledge of allegiance to Americas flag is offensive to Muslims and foreigners, and the word God has been displaced in every American icon. Traffic laws are being disregarded in cities like NY, where Muslims are allowed to block streets during Friday prayer (Jummah), Family courts across the country are losing power granting divorces as Muslims seek their own courts for such purposes and who knows what laws were broken when a Tennessee police officer allowed a vehicle to continue on its way after being advised there was a dead child in the trunk. (http://www.bizpacreview.com/2014/12/13/saudi-man-tells-police-he-has-permit-for-dead-child-in-his-trunk-officer-lets-him-go-165021)

All done in the name of political correctness.

Murder of "moderate" Muslim intellectuals who don't support Islamization. NA

Destruction of churches, synagogues and other non-Muslim institutions. NA• **Women are restricted further in accordance with Sharia law.** • **Large-scale destruction of population, assassinations, bombings.** NA

Toppling of government and usurpation of political power. NA

Imposition of Sharia Law: Every time an accommodation for a Muslim is met, sharia is imposed. From allowing prisoners to maintain their beards, (http://www.nydailynews.com/news/national/u-s-supreme-court-muslim-convicts-beards-article-1.2085315) removing meat products from school cafeterias,

(http://www.frontpagemag.com/2014/dgreenfield/muslims-halal-school-lunches-are-our-constitutional-right-2/) and imposing the call to prayer over an entire community

(http://www.americanthinker.com/blog/2015/01/muslim_call_to_prayer_blasted_out_over_ucla_.html)

These are just incremental, methodical ways we are submitting to sharia.

The mere fact ANY, ANY of the above is occurring should be an alarm for Americans to awaken. The Islamists are being empowered and emboldened as we allow them to change us from inside out. It is only a matter of time we are blasted out of our comfort zone, as they are warning us, they are here, and they will rise.

ARE AMERICANS WILLING TO SUBMIT TO ISLAM? YOU ALREADY ARE ...PART 4

S eems really farfetched doesn't it? After all this is America, we have the Constitution, and the Bill of Rights, we have laws and courts to enforce those laws. There are branches of government already in place, with a system that allows us to elect those to serve and protect our foundational principles. So what's the problem.

As you have witnessed over the last few years, the strength and leadership which has always defined what America is in the eyes of the world, is shaking at its core. With elements of Stage 3 already in place, hold on tight, Stage 4 isn't far behind. With the inhumanity of an Islamic group that has burned a human being alive, and a president that has publicly admonished Christians, what is left other than for the atrocities to begin occurring within our own borders.

Here are the elements to Stage 4. Bulleted points with "NA" means it is not occurring in the United States at this time that we are aware of.

STAGE 4: Totalitarian ISLAMIC "THEOCRACY"
Islam becomes the only religious-political-judicial-cultural ideology. The President of the United States openly disparages

Christians at National Prayer day, openly uses the term "our religion" when referring to Islam, and refers to a deadly, vile Islamic group as a "jv" team is just a seed of ideology that is spreading into every corner of America. Since the office of the President of the United States is embracing a Muslim political party (United States Council of Muslim Organizations), embracing the implementation of Sharia law in areas dominated with Muslims (Dearborn MI) and condones the refusal of Muslim refugees and immigrants to assimilate and accept our culture, it has begun. Welcome to stage 4.

Sharia becomes the "law of the land. "In 2013 during "Muslim Day" at the Capitol in Austin TX, their director of CAIR, Mustapha Carroll stated: "If we are practicing Muslims, we are above the law of the land."   The agenda is in place. • **All non-Islamic human rights cancelled.   NA**

Enslavement and genocide of non-Muslim population. NA

Freedom of speech and the press eradicated.   The OIC (Organization of Islamic Cooperation) has worked within the UN to draft UN Resolution 16/18, which calls for a defamation of religion law. Currently there is an uprising regarding just how free speech should be if it offends Muslims, Islam, or the prophet Mohammed. While free speech has not been eradicated, the wheels are in motion to limit speech if it is deemed hateful. But who will define hate?

All religions other than Islam are forbidden and destroyed. NA

Destruction of all evidence of non-Muslim culture, populations and symbols in country (Buddha's, houses of worship, art, etc.). NA

The House of Islam ("peace"), dar al-Islam, includes those nations that have submitted to Islamic rule, to Sharia law. The rest of the world is in the House of War, dar al-harb, because it does not submit to Sharia law, and exists in a state of rebellion or war with the will of 'Allah.' No non-Muslim state or its citizens are "innocent," and remain viable targets of war for not believing in 'Allah.' The Christian, Jewish, Copts, Hindus and Zoroastrian people of the world have suffered under subjugation for centuries. Dhimmis are forbidden to construct houses of worship or repair existing ones, economically crippled by the Jizya (tax), socially humiliated, legally discriminated against, and generally kept in a permanent state of weakness, fear and vulnerability by Islamic governments.

SO that is the final stage. Keep in mind in order to create the caliphate the number of Muslims must be high enough to assist in fully implementing their law. Also keep in mind the following.

The vast number of refugees being settled within the United States are from Islamic countries. (https://refugeeresettlement-watch.wordpress.com/2015/02/04/over-110000-iraqis-have-entered-the-us-since-the-end-of-the-bush-administration/)

(https://refugeeresettlementwatch.wordpress.com/2015/02/02/more-news-about-syrian-muslims-headed-to-kentucky/)

The current administration in the White House sympathizes and supports terrorist groups such as the Muslim Brotherhood, Hamas and CAIR. This administration in the White House has held meetings with members of the Muslim Brotherhood.

(http://www.jihadwatch.org/2015/01/obama-state--department-hosts-muslim-brotherhood-leaders)

The current administration in the White House is decimating the United States Military

The current administration in the White House wants to disarm the American people

The current administration in the White House is creating a welfare state, providing full benefits to foreigners, while leaving its middle class and military without jobs, and healthcare

Overall, the tone within the United States is extreme divisiveness, anger and frustration.

A sleeping giant is awakening. God bless America, God help us all.

THE INTERFAITH SCAM PART 1

J ust because the word "interfaith" indicates faith, doesn't necessarily mean yours, but you can be certain it does mean Islam. Interfaith is to our religious institutions like the words diversity and culture are to our Education system, a disguise called Dawa. Dawa is the proselytizing of Islam, an obligation that must be performed by all good Muslims. What is a good Muslim? To infidels or kafirs (all non-Muslims) it would be a pious person that ascribes to the doctrine of their religion, and is accepting, tolerant and respectful of fellow human beings. Not quite. A good Muslim will ascribe to their religious beliefs, which is summed up in the first pillar, the Shahada. "There is no god but Allah, and Mohammed is the Prophet". But looking deeper, they believe Islam is meant to dominate, not be dominated or equal to any other religion.

In a document called the "Methodology of Dawa" written by Shamim A. Siddiqui and published in 1989, the true objective is indisputably clear. There must be an Islamic Movement in the United States, and Dawa is the path to that goal. The below excerpts are from this book, and are some of the more revealing ones.

From the Introduction of the book (pg. 20) *"That is why, it is very important that a full-fledged Islamic Movement is established in the United States of America and elsewhere in Europe and Latin America to serve the greater interest of Islam, the Muslim world and humanity at large. This is a game of strategy. We have to find out and create new friends for Islam and its cause on the side of the enemy, inside and at the rear of the forces fighting against Islam and its emergence as a force anywhere in this world is a future reality of great magnitude."*

Interfaith is a game of strategy.

(pg. 21)*" A Muslim has to put all that he has either to change the society into an Islamic society or state or be perished for it. A Muslim has no other choice"*.

Society must be changed into an Islamic society

(pg. 58) *"Acting upon the foregoing process, the Islamic Movement will produce the team of workers which is essentially required to meet the following needs:*

1. *To accelerate the pace of Dawa Ilallah to a greater and greater number of people in order to bring more and more individuals to the fold of Allah(SWT) and increase the number of workers till the movement becomes a force to be reckoned with"*

The movement becomes a force to be reckoned with.

(pg.59) *"The workers of the Islamic Movement will have to mobilize a relentless war against immoral practices, drugs, pornography, alcoholism, racial discrimination, homosexuality, and other like these. They will have to educate the public opinion, warn the society about their horrible consequences and mobilize people's opinion through meet-the-people campaigns"*

Relentless war against immoral practices, such as homosexuality

(pg.59) *"In the initial stage there may not be any opposition to Dawa work. For some time, the Islamic Movement of America may have some smooth sailing. But with the increase in Dawa efforts, in the number of activities and growth of the strength of the organization, the anti-Islamic forces will take notice of the multifarious activities of the Movement."*

The multifarious activities of the Movement

(pg.60) *"Through this process, the Movement will penetrate deep into the hearts of the common folk, gain sympathy against oppression and generate a befitting counter-offensive campaign against the false propaganda of Batil. Simultaneously, the movement may also seek legal protection from the court for fundamental human rights to propagate what its adherents believe to be correct and to profess the same through democratic, peaceful and constitutional means"*

Penetrate deep into the hearts of common folk, and seek legal protection from the court

(pg. 109) *The Christian community of America will need a special approach to make them understand their misguided concept about Jesus (PBUH). Prophet Jesus (PBUH) was also a messenger of God, as others were. He was born without a father as a miracle of God. There is nothing spectacular in it, if we believe in God, in His absolute power and in His total control over the natural phenomenon. He can create anything just by ordering "Be" and "it is done." He created Jesus without a father. He created Adam without a father or a mother, and Eve without a mother. They do not ascribe the attributes of God to either one of them. How then, can they profess Jesus to be the Son of God. It is illogical and quite absurd. Jesus was a Prophet and a man. He had all the human needs and weaknesses. He ate food for his existence, slept for rest and did all the other things a human being needs for his survival. By their misconstrued conception innovated by St. Paul, Christians have made Jesus (PBUH) into a "Human-God." This is clear idolatry. Making partners with God is a sin. He will never forgive this sin.*

Each of these notions that have been captured in the first several chapters are evidence to the agenda, ideology and their position on the superiority of Islam. Interfaith = Dawa, not exactly the impression they believe all religions are equal. So to sum it up:

Interfaith is a game of strategy.
Society must be changed into an Islamic society
The movement becomes a force to be reckoned with
Relentless war against immoral practices, such as homosexuality (remember they have embraced the gay community)
The multifarious activities of the Movement
Penetrate deep into the hearts of common folk, and seek legal protection from the court
Misguided concept of Jesus, Professing Jesus to be the son of God is Illogical and absurd
So far, the facade the Islamic community portrays as being open and respectful of your religion is quite untrue.

THE INTERFAITH SCAM PART 2

T he Methodology of Dawa Is quite a find. As you read in part one of the Interfaith Scam, Dawa is simply the instrument Islamists use to convince others they are just like us, and their god is the same as ours. Well, no it's not.

The following excerpts are again from the last few chapters in the "Methodology of Dawa." Judge for yourself.

(pg. 117) *Prophets' day like Abraham's Day, Moses's Day, Jesus's Day and Muhammad's Day (Peace be upon all of them) will be organized and celebrated by the Islamic Movement on national scale with seminars and symposium all over the country. In these gatherings the religious leaders/scholars of Jewish and Christian communities will be invited to express their views freely. The speeches will be followed by an open discussion in a scholarly manner. This will provide a good opportunity to attract the Judeo-Christian community in great numbers and put the correct status of these Prophets before them in a historical perspective. It will be presented in a very academic atmosphere, with no aggressiveness at all under any circumstances. This discussion will crystallize the position of each prophet as the Prophet of Islam and the people will have a unique*

opportunity to understand Islam in its true historical background. This will pave the way to present Islam to these communities as a continuity of the message from the Creator, each Prophet proclaiming, "be obedient to God alone and shun the evil forces
   (Batil/Taghut)" (H.Q. 16:36).

   "Islam will thus be presented to them, not as something new but as the historical development of Judeo-Christian Islam which is neither traceable in the Torah nor in the Bible. The Qur'an will thus emerge as the only book of Guidance that bears the correct and up-to-date teachings of Islam and the life of Prophet Muhammad (PBUH) as the only model to humanity to follow. This will also provide the valuable opportunity to portray the life and teachings of all the previous prophets, whose life and teachings had been distorted in the Old and New Testaments, correctly. The version of the Qur'an about these prophets is the only authentic account of their lives now available to mankind."

"Islam will thus be presented to them, not as something new but as the historical development of Judeo-Christian Islam which is neither traceable in the Torah nor in the Bible."

(pg.119) Through Contacts With Churches, Synagogues, Colleges And Universities: These are very important public platforms that must be used for the spread of Dawa when available, either on the invitation or by offering the services of the Da'ee to these institutions for presenting the viewpoint of Islam on various issues of the time The religious dignitaries and the learned teachers of Universities and colleges will also be invited to speak in the arranged open Dawa programs of the Movement on various issues and topics of common interest. The speeches will be followed by open discussions and Question/Answer sessions. This will give an opportunity to the Da'ee to thrash out the issue and bring the discussion to the desired conclusion

"arranged open Dawa programs and bring the discussion to the desired conclusion"

> *(pg. 120) "Here in the educational institution, the teacher should be the top target. They are free, they have the time and they exert a lot of influence upon the students. If they are convinced about Islam as a way of life, they can motivate their students to that effect in great numbers. Teachers will therefore, be the special Dawa targets of the Islamic Movement"*

"they exert a lot of influence upon the students".

> *(pg128) "Service to humanity (to the common folk of the society) is perhaps one of the most effective means of communicating and delivering the message of Islam to the people."*
>
> *(pg.129) "Service to Elderly People There are about 60 million people who are above the age of 65 and retired from active service. Many of them are normally sick or incapacitated and confined to homes or elderly people care centers. They are a useful electorate"*

Service to Youth and Runaway Children- services will provide great opportunities for Dawa work among the neglected youth of the society.

"Reconciliation Service to Battered Families" This counseling service to battered husbands and battered wives will ultimately bring them nearer to Islam. They will all feel obliged to the teachings of Islam that changed their lives and made their matrimonial life happier and rejuvenated."

Dawa is equal to another dirty deed of society, called drug dealing. Supply those in need with what makes them feel good, and they become hooked.

THE DECEIT BEHIND THE INTERFAITH CURTAIN

The following are excerpts from" **INTERFAITH DIALOGUE AND WHAT JESUS SAYS: Points for Christians to Ponder before Engaging in Interfaith Dialogues,** a paper written by Matt Bonner, a friend and colleague of Dailyrollcall. Before participating in an Interfaith forum, one must understand the deceptive foundation on which it is built.

Section III
CONSIDER DIFFERING CODES OF ETHICS
Exploring the topics of dualistic ethics, Taqiyyah and Abrogation is critical to any discussion about Islam. Without clear understanding of these key concepts, it is impossible to grasp the reality of what we face when dialoguing with Muslims.

First, it is important to note that Islam denies the principle of the Golden Rule: the belief that all human beings are equal in value and should be treated the same. Love for the non-Muslim is simply not taught in their doctrine or in the Mosque. In fact, there are 25 verses in the Koran that discuss how Allah does not love kafirs (non-Muslims). There is not a single verse about compassion or love for the Kafir.

Islamic ethics are dualistic, which means there is one set of ethics for Muslims and another set for non-Muslims. Because of this dualistic worldview, there is no unified humanity, only a division between Muslims and Kafirs. In his book, Thirteen Lessons on Islam for Christians, Dr. Bill Warner writes, *"The term human being has no meaning inside of Islam. There is no such thing as humanity, only the duality of the believer and the kafir. In the ethical statements found in the Hadith, a Muslim should not lie, cheat, kill, or steal from other Muslims. But a Muslim may lie, deceive, or kill a kafir if it advances Islam."*

DUALISTIC ETHICS AND WORLDVIEW OF ISLAM

The dualistic worldview of Islam can also be explained by the way Islam divides the world into two realities: The Dar al-harb and the Dar al-Islam. The Dar al-harb is the house of war, the world of the sword, the infidel and perpetual war. Countries that are non-Muslim reside in the Dar al-harb. Dar al-Islam is the house of Islam, the land of Islam and peace. So here is where the truth of Islamic dualism really hits home: **Peace on earth does not come until the entire world has been made Dar al-Islam.** Read that sentence again.

This is an essential truth that all non-Muslims must understand. As a result of this worldview, Islam is under permanent jihad obligation to reduce the Dar al harb to non-existence. Consequently, pious Muslims have no allegiance to any country, state or government; they owe allegiance only to Mohammed's original ideology. They salute no flag and wear no uniform. Syed Qutb, one of the most influential Islamic theologians and leaders of the Muslim Brotherhood of the 20th Century said, "A Muslim has no nationality except his belief." It helps to understand that in Islamic teaching, all people will one day accept Islam or submit to its rule.

This also explains why Islam cannot recognize political borders or permanent peace treaties, and this precedent was set by Mohammed. He disregarded and nullified his ten-year treaty with the Meccans (The Treaty of AlHudaybiyah) after only two years, going on to conquer Mecca in 630 AD. In fact, Yasser Arafat referred to this treaty numerous times after signing the Oslo Accords in 1993. He said it was the basis of his peace with Israel. (Brigitte Gabriel 37-38) Lastly, we must understand that any act of war against Dar Al Harb is morally and legally justified, and exempt from any ethical judgment—according to Ibin Taamiyah, a 14th century Muslim Jurist (Brigitte Gabriel-2).

TAQIYYA

The Koranic concept of Taqiyya (rooted in Suras 16:106; 3:28; 2:225; 5:89) is an essential concept of deception to understand. Taqiyya is "sacred deception" or "legitimate deception" and is simply a lie or deception that advances Islam. It is not considered a sin. Acting friendly and welcoming to neighbors, while harboring hatred or disgust in the heart, is an example of Taqiyya. It is a way of disguising true feelings. The foundation for Taqiyya is found in the Hadith:

I did not hear him (the Prophet Muhammad) permit untruth in anything people say except for three things: war, settling disagreements, and a man talking with his wife or she with him. (Sacred Hadith, Muslim)

"Speaking is a means to achieve objectives . . . it is permissible to lie if attaining the goal is permissible . . . and obligatory to lie if the goal is obligatory." (Imam Abu Hamid Ghazali, renowned Islamic Jurist, quoted in Umdat al Salik, Sacred Islamic Law, Book R: Holding One's Tongue, r8.2)

In his book, The Mosque Exposed, former Islamic Jurist Sam Solomon writes:

Fakharadin A'razi states that if a Muslim fears those unbelievers amongst whom he may be because of their excessive power and strength, then he needs to pledge loyalty and love outwardly on condition that he inwardly would object to what he himself is saying; in other words, he would be saying the opposite to all that he inwardly believed. (pp. 58-64)

The significance of this tool bears some discussion and begs the question: **Why would we want to dialogue with people who are allowed, even encouraged, to lie and deceive us**? Can we trust anything they say or even the very premise of the dialogues? The result of this centuries-old practice is that not only do non-Muslims get deceived, but Muslims lie to each other all the time with permission from their doctrines. It is worth noting here that what drives the conscience of the Islamic world is shame and honor, not truth and fiction. It is far more important to maintain the outward appearance of honor, than it is to be truthful. Do we really want to subject ourselves to a dialogue with those who not only see lying as permissible, but who do so to advance Islam?

ABROGATION
Another key to Islamic deception is the legal concept of abrogation. Very simply, abrogation means that later verses of the Koran trump or overpower earlier verses. In other words, anything revealed to Mohammed chronologically later in the Koran, abrogates or overrules anything which came earlier. It is a way of allowing both to be true. In his book Thirteen Lessons on Islam for Christians, Dr. Bill Warner explains abrogation this way: Since Allah is perfect and the Koran is the exact words of Allah, then both contradictory verses are true. But the later verse is better or stronger than the earlier verse. This leads to dualistic logic where two contradictory facts can both be true.

Abrogation explains another reason Muslim clerics can cheerfully espouse the peaceful verses of the Koran. Inwardly, they know these verses have been abrogated, and they are counting on our ignorance and blind acceptance in the name of religious freedom. Abrogation comes from three verses in the Koran (Suras 17:106; 16:101; and 2:106) which state, "None of Our revelations do we abrogate or cause to be forgotten, but we substitute something better or similar; knowest thou not that Allah hath power over all things?"

Therefore, it is imperative that whenever a Muslim quotes a peaceful verse from the Koran, we ask him when it was revealed to Mohammed—in Mecca or in Medina? Then, kindly assure him that you understand the doctrinal practice of abrogation and that unfortunately, that verse has been abrogated by a stronger verse that came later.

COMMON CORES OTHER AGENDA PART ONE

Where does the real template for common core come from? Among the most talked about is Arne Duncan, and Bill Gates, but what about the not so talked about?

In August of 2013, Arne Duncan, the Secretary of Education and Sal Khan (Khan Academy) participated in a Google+ "hangout", where Duncan praised innovators such as Khan, stating *"Like Khan Academy, the Department of Education is continuing to work to innovate in education and secure that the next generation can have all the educational opportunities they deserve"*

Sal Khan, founder of the Khan Academy is an American born Muslim who developed a website that *"allows anyone, anywhere to take over 4,500 individual classes online, free of charge. across disciplines and academic grade levels, Khan Academy courses have allowed millions of individuals to learn something new".*

Duncan believes this is the new way of learning unlike the "Neanderthal" ways of the past.

http://www.whitehouse.gov/blog/2013/08/23/check-out-secretary-education-arne-duncans-google-hangout-sal-khan

Khan seems to be the new hot ticket, as he and Bank of America have partnered to offer online classes on financial matters. Khan also is the author of The One World Schoolhouse which Khan believes is a "virtual extension" of his philosophy.

Khan has been named the number 91 Muslim Hero according to the websitehttp://www.muslim-heroes.org/ where he joins the ranks of Sihajj Wahajj, Ahmed Bedier, Zahra Billoo and several other Muslims known for their radical, and sometimes terrorist organization connections. Khans is just one area the U.S Department of Education is experimenting with in using the internet to teach your children.

But it gets even scarier...

In 2011 The Qatar Foundation International, partnered with the Department of State and the U.S. Department of Education to promote a marriage between students in the U.S. and international schools through the "Connect All Schools" project. (http://www.qfi.org/page/105/5/iEARN-USA) The stated goal of this initiative is to connect every school in the United States to the world by 2016.

So while foreign countries are invading your child's classroom, grant money is pouring in to assure these programs will work. Two schools in Tucson AZ were recipients of $465,000 intended to implement "innovative curricula and teaching materials to be used in any Arabic language classroom". This is money that comes from a foundation with close ties to the Muslim Brotherhood, which is an offshoot of Hamas.

In 2012, public schools in Harlem NY were given $250,000 from the Qatar foundation for a pilot program in which students voluntarily learned Arabic, however this year, it will be mandatory for students in second grade through 5th grade to learn the language. Many are wondering why it's necessary.

Then there is the Qatar Foundations project in City Center DC. The 1,400-square-meter cultural center, called Al Bayt, (Arabic for "home"), which will feature "state of the art, interactive experience" which will engage students in Qatari culture "without leaving

the states". http://www.qatarchronicle.com/gulf-business/42521/
qatar-foundation-to-open-arab-cultural-centre-for-american-pu-
pils/ "Al Bayt will be a state of the art, interactive experience that
will immerse students in different aspects of the culture, language,
architecture, design and more." According to Sahar Al Ansari, he
will be featured as a "Virtual Ambassador" guiding people through
the space while demonstrating their different perspectives and experiences, as well as their similarities, to an American audience.
The ambassadors spoke about their language, religion, lifestyles,
family and the environment of their region and homes

Are you seeing a trend here?

Back on the home front, we see organizations such as the
Council on Islamic Education (CIE) which now goes by the
Institute on Religion and Civic Values. The Council on Islamic
Education was founded in 1991 to provide academic support and
scholarly resources about Islam and Muslim history to K-12 textbook publishers, educators, and others. One of those involved in
the research and writing of these books is Shabbir Mansuri who
has stated" I am waging a "bloodless" revolution, promoting world
cultures and faiths in America's classrooms".

The CIE (IRCV) is: The Leading contributor and consultant
to publishers of textbooks that include Islamic-related content
Promoting sanitized, inaccurate information about Islam in K-12
education and has associations with the Islamic Saudi Academy,
the Council on American-Islamic Relations (CAIR), and the
Islamic Circle of North America (ICNA), front groups for the anti-Christian, anti-American, and anti-Israel Muslim Brotherhood

Mansuri also has 2 articles published on **Soundvision.com**, an
Islamic resource website often referred to educators as the "go to"
site for Islamic education materials.

The 2 articles are

ISLAM: How to Get Religious Accommodation in The Public School
System: A Six-Step Guide and Muslim Schools VS. Public Schools.

COMMON CORES OTHER AGENDA PART 2

Susan Douglass is a convert to Islam from Virginia who is the principle researcher and writer for CIE (Council for Islamic Education). Douglas has taught social studies at the controversial Islamic Saudi Academy (ISA), an academy which has been cited for using textbooks that condemn Jews and Christians as infidels and enemies of Islam. She also was an attendee at a meeting in April of 2001 at the White House under George Bush, that brought together key Muslim Brotherhood figures, some of which are currently in prison for aiding or financing terrorists.

If that isn't bad enough, Douglas also is responsible for editing numerous manuscripts of world history textbooks used by middle and high school students across America, advises state education boards on curriculum standards dealing with world religion and has helped train thousands of public school teachers on Islamic instruction.

Another group that has its hand in education via a back door is ING (Islamic Network Group) founded by Egyptian Maha El Genadi. ING states it is a non-profit organization whose mission is to counter prejudice and discrimination against American

Muslims by teaching about their traditions and contributions in the context of America's history and cultural diversity

Their curricula, which is listed on their website, contains:

Muslims and their faith: Getting to Know American Muslims and Their Faith

A History of Muslims in America: Muslim Contributions to Civilization

All this is designed to supplement content standards in social studies and world history and addresses state social studies content standards of leading states

The ludicrous contents of this sort of curricula even goes so far to suggest perhaps Columbus didn't discover America, but rather the Muslims did. This from their website:

Lesson One: Muslims and America, A Long History:
The first lesson emphasizes the fact that Muslims are not new to America, but came here along with early European explorers and settlers
Lesson Two: Before Columbus:
This lesson explores the possibility of Muslims having preceded Columbus to the New World

To best sum up ING, www.tn4politicaljustice.wordpress.com writes this about ING:

Given the organizational affiliations of ING Board members and its founder, Ms. ElGanaidi's documented appearances with CAIR national leadership and appearances at Muslim Brotherhood ISNA's conferences, and the written affirmations of standing partnerships between ING and Muslim Brotherhood named organizations, the ING approach makes sense.

The recent May 5, 2012 ING Program in California included a book signing by the former imam of the Ground Zero mosque, Imam Feisal Abdul Rauf and a detailed report by ING President, Ms. ElGanaidi's. Page 5 of her report states (emphasis added):

> "[ING has] also received letters of support from national organizations which reflects our partnerships and good relations with these organizations as well as our reach across the country. These include: Islamic Circle of North America (ICNA), Muslim American Society (MAS), Islamic Society of North America (ISNA)and the Council on Islamic Relations – California (CAIR)"

ISNA's letter of support attached at page 24 of Ms. ElGanaidi's report states:

> "We have seen the positive impact of these projects on our community through our years of work with ING, especially during the Annual ISNA Convention, and training webinars, which we were proud to co-sponsor with ING."

So Common Core is a set of consistent education standards being implemented across the states. Consistent for whom? With all the back door infiltrations of Islamist groups and ideologies, it's not consistent with the principles or ideology of America. No longer will children be treated as individuals who learn to have pride and love of our country, but rather a group that is being prepared for a global society.

Sometimes you have to read in between the lines.

DENY ALL YOU WANT, INDOCTRINATION IS IN PUBLIC SCHOOLS.

"Facts do not cease to exist because they are ignored."
Indoctrination is a process where a seed is planted, and if nurtured, ultimately leads to radicalization. Textbooks are only one vehicle, a growing presence of radical organizations in schools are another.

The Muslim Student Association, a Muslim Brotherhood front group, entered college campuses in 1963 at the University of Illinois, Urbana. Their purpose is to perform dawa, (proselytizing of Islam) which is every good Muslims religious obligation. Previously limited to colleges and universities, they are now rearing their heads in high schools. In Davidson County TN, Martin Luther King Magnet School was the first, and Now Hume Fogg is the latest.

Throughout Tennessee students in public schools have been exposed to the doctrine of Islam by attending field trips to mosques which at the end of the day, Qurans were set out for students to take, pork products were banned from Sunset Elementary in Brentwood TN, children in the Rutherford County schools received gifts from a Muslim student for Eid al Fitr and third graders were given hand-outs written by the Nation of Islam. Nothing historical, just religion and sharia.

It isn't by coincidence Muslim children are attending public schools, they are another way in which the word of Islam is spread. In an article on the Muslim Brotherhood websitehttp://www.Soundvision.com (http://www.soundvision.com/article/sharing-islam-dawa-in-public-schools) it states:

Muslim parents have the option to send their children to Islamic schools. Just as Christians and Jews that want their children to be exposed to an environment that adheres to their religious doctrines and values sends them to their private religious schools. In another article from Soundvision.com, Ibrahim Bowers, the author of "Monitoring Public Schools, what are They Teaching My Kid" (http://www.soundvision.com/article/monitoring-public-schools-what-are-they-teaching-my-kids) clearly dislikes the public school system:

> *"The loss of their Islamic identity is a terrible price to pay for their learning to read English, add two and two, and attend public school in America."*

The only reason Islamists insist Islam be a part of public school student's curriculum, is the same reason the Islamists send their children to public schools. To perform a religious duty, dawa, and to plant the seed of Islam in their head, indoctrination.

Dawa in public schools
Schools are therefore fertile grounds where the seeds of Islam can be sowed inside the hearts of non-Muslim students. Muslim students should take ample advantage of this opportunity and present to their schoolmates the beautiful beliefs of Islam.

From (http://www.soundvision.com/article/sharing-islam-dawa-in-public-schools):

The bottom line
We should use every opportunity to sensitize non-Muslim peers and school staff to Islam and to establish an environment in which everywhere a non-Muslim turns, he notices Islam portrayed in a positive way, is influenced by it and eventually accepts Islam with Allah's guidance, Insha Allah (if God wills).
Indoctrination pure and simple.

THE MYTH OF ISLAMOPHOBIA, THE TRUTH ABOUT THOSE WHO INVENTED IT.

Muslims across America are demanding Islamophobia be stopped by creating a false rise in what they consider anti-Muslim rhetoric. Islamophobia is a word manufactured by the Muslim Brotherhood in an effort to invent a false sense of victimhood. Islamophobia is defined by Muslims as those who hold an irrational fear of Islam, and is seen as a mental deficiency.

The word itself means a fear of Islam, but the word has morphed into meaning a hatred of Muslims, racism, or bigotry. It encompasses negative words that cause discomfort and embarrassment, thereby causing people to think twice about speaking negatively about Islam and Muslims. Being labelled a hater or racist (which Islam is not a race) can get you fired, lose family and friends, or lose business. All fears of the American people.

Islamic organizations like the Council on American Islamic Relations (CAIR) have created a sense of urgency in hopes the government will step in by criminalizing what they consider hate speech. Incidents have been fabricated to make it appear there is a spike in anti-Muslim sentiment which in turn they say promotes violence, vandalism and hate.

Aside from the fear of being labeled an islamophobe, people are shying away from anything that may be construed as islamophobic and instead flooding to hear Muslims preach about Islam, its peaceful and loving nature, its tolerance of all things sinful, and how compatible sharia law is to the constitution (all untrue)

HOWEVER, the most important point is not about Islamophobia but rather how it is being used by Muslims. Their efforts to end Islamophobia have instead created a national security risk.

Law enforcement and our military have become so delicate to Muslim communities for fear of losing federal funding or their pensions they are cooperating with Muslim communities conducting business in a way that doesn't offend the Muslims. Because of the demands by Muslims to further their agenda and our political correctness, some of the outcomes of these implications are:

The purging of relevant, factual training that includes who terrorist organizations and their supporters are within the US, The termination of surveillance in mosques

The end of profiling, the ceasing of standard search procedures, such as canines to detect explosives, the barring of our military being able to identify the enemy and annihilate them, the altering of rules of engagement replaced with recall and retreat, and the cessation of interrogation tools that are effective but are seen as offensive and demeaning

All because Muslims label these Islamophobic. All of these things we have viewed as small incremental changes, are now the result of our law enforcement agencies calling Islamic terrorism acts of domestic extremism.

By not immediately designating killings such as San Bernardino, Chattanooga, Fort Hood or Garland TX as Islamic terrorism, they are falling into criminal categories rather than terrorist ones. We are becoming desensitized to the reality of an enemy who is fighting in the name of Islam that has an ideology that is dismantling and destroying America.

It isn't Islamophobia that is dangerous, it is those calling for its demise who are

MUSLIMS SAY ISLAMOPHOBIA IS BEHIND REFUGEE DENIAL

Muslims say Islamophobia is why Americans are opposing 10,000 Syrians entering the United States. Never mind the Islamic terror group ISIS has stated they will pose as refugees to enter this country. Disregard the warnings directly from ISIS leaders they are coming. Dismiss the fears from our largest law enforcement agency, the FBI, who states ISIS has cells in every state. Really.

The insistence and determination by the Muslims in America to demand 10,000 Syrian refugees enter the United States is disturbing and very telling. Woven throughout their own stories of woeful victimization, are lectures and anecdotes chastising those who oppose the refugees at this time due to lack of proper vetting. It has become very clear, the Muslim communities in America do not care about the safety and security of our nation.

Once again, the truth has been perverted to align with their agenda. The outspoken and opposed are belittled and made to somehow feel guilty. Pictures of babies, children and mothers are posted across social media rather than the real refugees, who are predominately males, well built and defiant.

Yes, America was once a melting pot, accepting of those in need and suffering. Yes, we took in the tired, the poor and huddled masses, but those were different times. Not only was the horrific violence from terrorists nonexistent, but refugees and immigrants came here, not to do harm, and destroy our foundation, but to assimilate, and become proud Americans.

Yes, the culture and traditions of ethnic groups were practiced among their communities, yes there were pockets of neighborhoods where they resided and became entrepreneurs, like Little Italy and Chinatown. But they were patriotic, they loved America and all it stood for. They spoke the language, and were proud of what they accomplished.

Muslims in America are quite the contrary. Muslim neighborhoods have become no go zones in now Muslim majority cities. Muslims decry freedom of speech, defining it as hate or Islamophobia if it is in opposition to their beliefs and ideas. Muslims demand accommodations to fulfill their religious obligations, but yet take offense to others. Muslims command respect, yet give none. Muslims want to implement their laws, which are completely antithetical to ours. Muslims want to indoctrinate our children, rather than assimilate their own. Muslims want their rights but take away yours. Muslims want to celebrate their holidays, but are offended by Christmas and Easter. Muslims seek attention for all their good deeds, and they take over streets so you can see them pray. Muslims want to live in America, but are unhappy they do.

Muslims in America may not desire to join violent Islamic groups, but they don't appear to possess the strength to fight them either. Condemnation is easy from a keyboard.

At such a volatile time in America, I agree and support those that have taken a stand to protect Americans from a siege that is sure to follow once these refugees are settled within our borders.

America was founded on Judaea Christian principles and religion but other religions have been embraced and have thrived because there was no political agenda. At no time in history has a "religion" sought to take over America, to change the very fabric which made it so great.

This is America, let's stop apologizing for it.

WILL TODAY BE THE BEGINNING OF THE END OF FREE SPEECH?

G et ready America, the terrorist organization the Council on American Islamic Relations (CAIR), is welcoming a congressional resolution H.Res.569, which condemns what they define as anti-Muslim bigotry, hate, and violence against Muslims in America.

In part: "Whereas the victims of anti-Muslim hate crimes and rhetoric have faced physical, verbal, and emotional abuse because they were Muslim or believed to be Muslim;

"Whereas the constitutional right to freedom of religious practice is a cherished American value and violence or hate speech towards any American community based on their faith is in contravention of our founding principles;

"Whereas there are millions of Muslims in the United States, a community made up of many diverse beliefs and cultures, and both immigrants and native-born Americans. . .

"Resolved, That the House of Representatives—

"(1) Expresses its condolences for the victims of anti-Muslim hate crimes;

"(2) Steadfastly confirms its dedication to the rights and dignity of all its citizens of all faiths, beliefs, and cultures

(Entire resolution is at the bottom of this page)

Rep. Don Beyer (D-VA) and some of his colleagues feel this step is necessary to put an end to anything anti -Muslim, "We must show that we will not tolerate this anti-Muslim discrimination and that those who propagate it do not represent the melting-pot America that we celebrate"

Wake up folks. This is undoubtedly the precursor to making any speech against Islam a crime. In the Islamic world it is known as a "Blasphemy Law", and in some countries, it is punishable by death.

The Islamophiles within our government are laying the foundation for our own demise. On December 12, 2015, the CAIR-Hamas political party, the United States Council of Muslim Organizations (USCMO) will be announcing its plans to stop Islamophobia.

Two United States Congressmen, Keith Ellison (MN) and Andre Carson (IN) will undoubtedly be present, as they not only co-sponsored the resolution, they have openly supported this Islamic political party.

Yes, this is the United States of America, yes this is the Muslim Brotherhood, oh and yes, we are in danger.

House Resolution 569 (https://www.congress.gov/bill/114th-congress/house-resolution/569)

Condemning violence, bigotry, and hateful rhetoric towards Muslims in the United States.

Whereas the victims of anti-Muslim hate crimes and rhetoric have faced physical, verbal, and emotional abuse because they were Muslim or believed to be Muslim;

Whereas the constitutional right to freedom of religious practice is a cherished American value and violence or hate speech towards any American community based on their faith is in contravention of our founding principles;

Whereas there are millions of Muslims in the United States, a community made up of many diverse beliefs and cultures, and both immigrants and native-born Americans;

Whereas this Muslim community is recognized as having made innumerable contributions to the cultural and economic fabric and well-being of American society;

Whereas hateful and intolerant acts against Muslims are contrary to the American values of acceptance, welcoming, and fellowship with those of all faiths, beliefs, and cultures;

Whereas these acts affect not only the individual victims but also their families, communities, and the entire group whose faith or beliefs were the motivation for the act;

Whereas Muslim women who wear hijabs, headscarves, or other religious articles of clothing have been disproportionately targeted because of their religious clothing, articles, or observances;

Whereas the rise of hateful and anti-Muslim speech, violence, and cultural ignorance plays into the false narrative spread by terrorist groups of Western hatred of Islam, and can encourage certain individuals to react in extreme and violent ways;

Resolved, That the House of Representatives—

Expresses its condolences for the victims of anti-Muslim hate crimes;

> Steadfastly confirms its dedication to the rights and dignity of all its citizens of all faiths, beliefs, and cultures;
> Denounces in the strongest terms the increase of intimidation, violence, vandalism, arson, and other hate crimes targeted against mosques, Muslims or those perceived to be Muslim;
> Recognizes that the Muslim community in the United States has made countless positive contributions to our society;

Declares that the civil rights and civil liberties of all United States citizens, including Muslims in the United States, should be protected and preserved;

Urges local and Federal law enforcement authorities to work to prevent hate crimes; and to prosecute to the fullest extent of the law those perpetrators of hate crimes; and

Reaffirms the inalienable right of every citizen to live without fear and intimidation, and to practice their freedom of faith.

UPDATE WILL TODAY BE THE BEGINNING OF THE END OF FREE SPEECH?

When will we learn Islam is not a religion but rather a complete, political way of life. The announcement made in January by the United States Council of Muslim Organizations (USCMO) regarding Islamophobia certainly defines their purpose. As referenced earlier in the article titled "Will Today Be the Beginning of the End of Free Speech", the USCMO released their objectives to curtail what they consider bigotry, and hate.

"Proposed USCMO initiatives include a drive to register one million voters prior to the 2016 presidential election, a "One America" campaign to enhance understanding of American Muslims and Islam and a "National Open Mosque Day" designed to help increase interactions between American Muslims and citizens of other faiths and backgrounds".

Registering one million voters isn't to cure Islamophobia, but rather to sway an election to the candidate they feel will best suit their agenda. Hillary Clinton was Secretary of State when the Organization of Islamic Cooperation (OIC) drafted a" Defamation of Religion Law" with help from the UN. The USCMO also has stated they would have the ability to sway elections in several key states in 2016.

Then there is the dawa. Spreading the word of Islam is a religious obligation, interfaith forums and invitations to mosques are just that.

"Another initiative planned by the national Muslim coalition includes the formation of new and strengthened alliances with interfaith partners, social justice groups and other minority communities that have faced or continue to face similar challenges."

And then there is victim-hood: "The USCMO will also seek to increase emergency preparedness for Islamic institutions and individual Muslims to address the rising number of hate incidents nationwide."

"USCMO member organizations discussed the real and present threat of violent extremist groups that are preying on young people via the Internet and who twist the meaning of the Quran to justify their atrocities."

"It was noted that groups such as Daesh (ISIS) kill more Muslims than they do people of other faiths"

And then the blame: "The coalition committed itself to combat all forms of violent extremism in the homeland. Experts in the field shared some factors related to radicalization that include isolation, the presentation of a twisted religious ideology and toxic anti-Muslim political rhetoric and negative perceptions of American policy, particularly in the Middle East. "

Words are important too. In the above statement, Muslims commit to combat forms of "violent extremism", not **Jihad.**

"These strategies will seek to prevent the targeting of members of the American Muslim community by those espousing extremist ideologies and will help young people to rejoin the mainstream community."

Not the American community.
"In each of the initiatives, coalition members will seek to protect the civil liberties of all Americans."

Will seek to protect, not will protect.
The Muslim Brotherhood has said their goal is one religion, one law and one government. The United States Council of Muslim Organization (USCMO) says One God, one vision, one voice. They are telling you they are here, what is there not to believe?

Read entire announcement here: http://www.uscmo.org/

HOW THE WEST WAS WON...? NO... LOST

It's a vicious cycle. The freedom of speech afforded to Americans allows for speaking and expressing what we believe to be the truth about Islam. In return, freedom of speech allows for the Muslims to negate and deny those truths by labeling us as haters, bigots and Islamophobes. Evens out right? Not quite. Islamist organizations and their supporters across the country are attempting to redefine freedom of speech by saying anything negative about their religion or their prophet is offensive, and should be labeled as hate speech. But who will define hate speech?

According to their doctrine, speaking ill of the prophet is considered blasphemy. Blasphemy in some Middle Eastern countries constitutes death. Will we Americans have to fear death for our freedom of speech? Not yet anyways.

In order to raise awareness to their plight of how any negative freedom of speech affects them, the tendency to play victim has become the new trend. Creating false incidents and narratives serves as the goal to gain sympathy and support, which in turn has the potential to pressure law makers to create policies to protect them. But it doesn't end there. Muslims claiming Islamophobia or hate speech has created a dire risk of their own genocide, which then becomes a human rights issue, which in turn becomes a U.N interest. This is how our freedom of speech will cease to exist as we know it.

In their own words in a website called Caliphate Online (http://www.caliphate.eu/2009/04/islams-view-towards-free-dom-of-speech.html) the author (AK) states in an article titled Islam's View Towards Freedom of Speech "Freedom of speech is a western concept that completely contradicts Islam. In reality there is no such thing as absolute free speech. What exists is speech within predefined limits that differ between nations. Nowadays freedom of speech is used as a colonial tool in the Muslim world to support the propagation of western ideas and to suppress Islamic ideas".

In 2008, the United States was a strong opponent to the UN's creation of a defamation of religion law citing the First Amendment was not compatible with such wording and further stated:

The U.S. Constitution and Supreme Court jurisprudence protect religious liberty while promoting tolerance and free speech. The introduction of "defamation of religions" laws would upset the delicate and successful-balance that has been achieved between the free exercise of religion and free speech, both of which are protected under the First Amendment. Government intrusion into these areas is unwarranted in the absence of a compelling purpose. Protecting the hurt feelings of aggrieved members of particular religious denominations is not one such purpose (http://www. heritage.org/research/reports/2008/11/why-the-us-should-op-pose-defamation-of-religions-resolutions-at-the-united-nations)

However, in 2011, an interesting rendition was accepted by the US, as it changed the verbiage previously used. "Earlier this year (2011) Western countries and their Latin American allies joined Muslim and African states in backing a new approach that switched the focus from protecting beliefs to protecting believers. Instead of a "Defamation of Religion Law, it is a "Resolution on

Combating Intolerance and Violence against Persons Based on Religion or Belief," Then Secretary of State Hillary Clinton stated "The United States strongly supports today's resolution, which rejects the broad prohibitions on speech called for in the former 'defamation of religions' resolution, and supports approaches that do not limit freedom of expression or infringe on the freedom of religion."

But they aren't giving up. In 2013, the OIC (Organization of Islamic Cooperation) released a new report on the rise of Islamophobia in the West to prove the existence of a "culture of intolerance of Islam and Muslims" citing the allowance of offensive and derogatory depictions of Islam and the prophet cause incitement, hence a propensity for violence against "believers".

Organizations such as the Muslim Brotherhood/Hamas supported CAIR (Council on American Islamic Relations) continue to label every confrontation, incident, or event as anti-Muslim, hateful, or Islamophobic. All in an effort to silence those educating the masses on the truth of Islam.

Will the Islamists win the battle to end free speech? Only if we close our eyes and hope it goes away like the monster underneath the bed.

HIZB-UT-TAHRIR...ANOTHER TERRORIST GROUP IN AMERICA

Amongst the Muslim Brotherhood, Al- Shabaab, and other groups here to inflict harm, Americans better wake up to yet another one. Hizb-ut-Tahrir

How is it such a subversive, incendiary group not just exists within our borders, but thrives. While many of their conferences have been relocated due to hotels not succumbing to their radical propaganda, the fact they exist still is troublesome. A pamphlet was handed out by members of this group in the last few years, which clearly shows their intentions and barbaric nature.

The Islamic Reformation pamphlet states:

"Apostasy is a question of what kind of person would openly and publicly abandon Islam with full knowledge that they will be killed for it, rather than either keeping it to themselves or leave the Khilafah. Hence, the death penalty only applies on those who in the Khilafah openly leave Islam, and choose to remain in the state despite knowing the law; this is considered an open attack on the basis of the state which is Islam, essentially it is viewed as treason and a political attack on the Khilafah in order to undermine it."

Oh yes, this is peaceful, and normal.

The following points are from their own website, and sums up their goals for America.

(http://www.hizbuttahrir.org/)

Hizb ut-Tahrir is a political party whose ideology is Islam. Its objective is to resume the Islamic way of life by establishing an Islamic State that executes the systems of Islam and carries its call to the world.

With regard to Hizb ut-Tahrir being a political party, this is because politics in Islam is looking after the affairs of the Ummah, domestically and externally and Allah (swt) has commanded the governing of the Ummah's affairs by Islam and nothing else.

Hizb ut-Tahrir has also determined its method of progress in view of the fact that Islam is an idea and a method, i.e. a host of tangible rules that preserve the idea and bring it into existence. Its method of progress is in fact the method of the Messenger of Allah (saw), for it is a group of clear and defined Sharia's rules. The party proceeds in the three periods, which the Messenger of Allah (saw) proceeded in order to achieve his objective:

1. The period of study and culture in order to generate the party culture and incorporate the ideology in a groups of individuals, i.e. in order to form the bloc.
2. The period of interaction with the Ummah and the struggle for the sake of making her adopt the ideology of the party as her own, make it her raison d'être and work towards establishing it.
3. The period of attaining and seizing the reins of power through the Ummah in order to implement the ideology in a comprehensive manner, because it is forbidden to seize partial power. Hence, the arrival at the ruling must be total and the implementation of Islam must be comprehensive.

Hizb ut-Tahrir is determined to work within the Ummah in order to implement Islam and achieve its objective by endeavoring to gain the leadership of the Islamic Ummah so that she could accept it as her leader, to implement Islam upon her and proceed with it in her struggle against the Kafir and in the work towards the return of the Islamic State as it was before, the leading superpower in the world.

It doesn't take much to equate the actions of Islamists around the state, or the country. Several positions in the political arena are being sought after by them, and because of their tenacity and efforts such as "getting the vote out", their collectiveness will most likely be one that reflects in the polls.

America has been dealt distraction after distraction. Americans have lost their jobs, their insurance and soon their freedoms. The last thing American families want to think about is organizations that are present to do further harm and destruction to our way of life.

This complacency and the affinity to be tolerant is a danger to every single one of us. Are you afraid of these groups and their ideology? You better be.

TWO OF MANY, ISLAMBERG IN HANCOCK NY AND ISLAMVILLE IN DOVER TN: WHY DO WE ALLOW THEM TO EXIST?

A Tennessee man has been arrested on terrorism charges for allegedly plotting to raid and destroy a Muslim terror training camp in NY. Robert Doggart from Signal Mountain TN, had formed what authorities are calling a militia with the intent to annihilate buildings and Muslims that live on a compound called Islamberg. While we don't condone the actions of Mr. Doggart, we do condemn the inactions of law enforcement and elected officials that have completely swept the existence of Islamberg under the rug.

In a telephone interview with WND, Delaware County NY Sheriff Craig DuPont states he did not believe the group called the Muslims of America to be a threat. This in great contrast to what the former Mayor of Deposit NY had to say, as well as the Deposit NY Police Dept., both expressing their concern for the unknown activities occurring.

Once again the focus Is being steered away from another very real concern, which is why Islamberg is allowed to exist given the documentation of who these Muslims really are. So who are they?

Currently there are 36 Jamaats, or "communities of the impoverished". Often, as in the case of Islamberg, they are in extremely remote areas, with mobile homes, a mosque, and a school. Some of the residents of Islamberg have resided there for years, while a vast number having been released from prison and are "reverts". They fall under the umbrella of Muslims of America, but their allegiance is to Sheikh Syed Mubarik Ali Shah El-Gilani aka Sheikh Gilani. Gilani, from Lahore Pakistan is the founder and leader of Jamaat Ul Fuqra, a violent, radical group with ties to Al Qaida, and was responsible for the 2002 beheading of Wall Street reporter Daniel Pearl. Khalid Sheik Mohammed, who was Osama Bin Laden's third in command, personally took responsibility for his beheading. Daniel Pearl was on his way to meet Gilani regarding the relationship of Richard Reid (the shoe bomber) with Al Qaida, when he was abducted.

Islamberg, whose sign reads the "International Quranic Open University" is active, and growing. And yes it is a danger to our country.

During our last visit to this compound, (which we never were invited in) we met two women who inadvertently stated it was "women's weekend" and they were tired from training. The conversation ended when pressed on what "training" they were referring to.

The existence of this "camp" is due in part they use religion as their ruse. They use "interfaith" as a shield and as always their mantra is we all have the same god. What law enforcement agency wants to be the first to raid a "religious community", undoubtedly their federal funding will come to a halt, and all will be labeled haters, bigots or Islamophobes. But how long does law enforcement look the other way? How long can the almighty dollar reign over conscience and duty to protect and serve? Where are the elected officials?

They may greet you with smiles and handshakes, but as former deceased leader Mummar Khadafy of Libya often said, they don't need bombs and guns to take over the west, they shall come from within.

Bingo

THE ISLAMISTS AND BLACK LIVES MATTER, SPRING OF 2016

"Why can't we have a revolution in America"
Khalilah Sabra, Muslim America Society

This is why there will be turmoil leading to November 2016.

Despite its peaceful name, the conference hosted by the Muslim Brotherhood group Muslims for America (MAS), titled" Muhammed, Peace Be upon Him, Mercy to Mankind', is anything but. Held every year in Chicago, last year's conference set a different tone. With speakers such as Tariq Ramadan, grandson of the founder of the Muslim Brotherhood, and CAIR's Hamas supporter Nihad Awad, their message is one everyone should hear.

In a six-minute video released by the Center for Security Policy Called "Star Spangled Sharia or a Muslim Brotherhood Revolution", radicals from various Muslim Brotherhood groups share their beliefs that the Black Lives Matters movement is their cause, they are the same.

Oussama Jammal, the Secretary General of the Muslim Brotherhood political party the United States Council of Muslim Organizations states "We will make every attempt to mobilize the community and put it on the political map, and therefore we will be the defenders of the Constitution of the United States of America".

Khalilah Sabra, of the Muslim American Society believes "We need to make a conscience decision to ourselves that black lives matter. Right now, we are feeling the effects of religious racism and intolerance that we have not seen in one hundred years. Basically, you are the black people of America, you are the people being imprisoned, you are the people being denied rights, you are the people being denied the dream."

Sabra further states," And just as these black brothers and sisters have been murdered in the streets, if we don't stand, you will see Muslims murdered in the streets."

Probably the most inciting statement in Sabra's speech was "We are the community that staged a revolution across the world. If we could do that, why can't we have that revolution in America."

It doesn't get any clearer. The Muslims want a revolution in America, however it won't be the Muslims doing the dirty work. They have chosen to embrace radical black groups that continue to deliver a message that is based on lies. "Hands up don't shoot", which came from the shooting of Michael Brown in Ferguson, has been the mantra, but is false. The Council of Islamic American Relations (CAIR) joined forces with Black Lives Matter to help promote these lies. Another lie circulating on social media, and driven by Muslims, is Americans voting to have Muslims banned from entering the United States. This, taken from, and out of context by a statement made by presidential candidate Donald Trump, where he suggested Muslims not be allowed to cross our borders until the government can properly vet refugees and develop a way to ensure terrorists are not among them.

A member of the Black Lives Matter group has posted on social media a graph of the percentage of voters that want to ban Muslims from entering the United States making it appear it was a question on the ballot. This wasn't on any ballot, this isn't a question being asked of voters, this is a blatant lie spread by a Black Lives Matter member.

Meanwhile, another radical director of CAIR, Hassan Shibly of Tampa FL, and a staunch supporter of Bernie Sanders, brags about being at the White House. CAIR states on its Face Book page that Hassan Shibly and other important members of the Muslim community in the U.S, met today with Senior White House officials, to discuss important American Muslim topics.

CAIR has joined forces with the Black Lives Matter group, CAIR has been designated a terrorist organization in the United Arab Emirates (UAE) and CAIR has been found to be an unindicted co-conspirator in the United States' largest terrorist funding trial held in Dallas TX called the Holy Land Foundation trial. The pieces of the puzzle are coming together.

An administration that has divided the country, hosting groups that want to dismantle it, who in turn are embracing those that will cause destruction and chaos.

Hold on America, here it comes.

GLOSSARY OF TERMS

A

Aisha: The daughter of Abu Bakr. She was Muhammad's third and favorite wife whom he married after the death of Khadijah, his first wife. Aisha was only six years old at the time of her marriage to Muhammad

Allah: God in Islam

Allah Akbar: God is great

As-salamu alaykum: Muslim greeting meaning peace be upon you

B

Batil: Falsehood

Bismillah al rahman al Rahim: "In the name of God, most Gracious, most Compassionate".

Burqa: An example of "full hijab", it is an enveloping outer garment worn by Muslim women for the purpose of hiding her body when out in public. (some Islamic governments make it a requirement).

C

Caliphs: The head of state in a Caliphate, and the title for the leader of the Islamic Ummah (body of Muslim believers). According to Islamic theology, the first four successors of Muhammad were the "Rightly-Guided Caliphs"

Caliphate: Refers to the first system of governance established in Islam, headed by Muhammad's companions, the Rightly-guided Caliphs

D

Dawa: Preaching; the missionary call to Islam; request to join Islam, and also the last ultimatum before 'legitimate' conquest by force. Proselytizing. Dawa is a religious obligation.

Dawah Ilallah - Calling the people to the fold of Allah

Da'ee Ilallah - One who calls to the fold of Allah **D.I.** - DATE ILALLAH

Deen: Religion

Dhimmi: Non-Muslim communities living under Islamic law (Sharia), who enjoy legal status but are subject to many restrictions and taxes. Also described as humans of second class, referring to the 'People of the Book', i.e. Jews and Christians.

E

F

Five Pillars: Compulsory for all Muslims. The pillars are, the shahada, salah, zakat, saum and hajj.

G

Good: To be good for a Muslim is to submit to Allah's will and then follow the 'right' path established by the examples set by the Prophet, and as such can differ to the popular understanding of the word.

H

Hadith: The Hadith are traditions of Muhammad, giving us important information about his life. They are usually narrations about a certain incident in which he said or did something. This is how Muslims determine the Sunnah (Muhammad's way of life.) It is key to Islam since Muslims are commanded to obey Muhammad and emulate him. In fact, four out of five of Islam's Pillars would not exist without the Hadith, therefore making Islam impossible to practice.

Haq: truth in Islam

Hajj: Annual (and often dangerous) pilgrimage to the Kaaba in Mecca

Halal: What is permitted if not mandatory. It defines all that is good or acceptable for a Muslim.

Haram: (opposite of halal); sinful; unlawful; forbidden

Hijab: a traditional scarf worn by Muslim women to cover the hair and neck and sometimes the face

Hijra: Due to growing animosity between the pagan and Muslim Meccans in 622 AD, Muhammad and his followers fled to Medina, marking the beginning of the Hijra (Migration) era of the Islamic lunar calendar and Muhammad's metamorphosis from a preacher to a political and military leader.

Ikhwan: Another word for Muslim Brotherhood

Infidel: a person who does not accept the Islamic faith; kaffir.

Insha allah: God willing

Iqamatuddeen: - A Qur'anic terminology for introducing, spreading and establishing the Deen of Allah

I M 0 A: Islamic movement of America

I M: Islamic movement

J

Jihad: Most often referring to the waging of wars of aggression and conquest against non-Muslims in order to bring them and their territories under Islamic rule.

Jizya: tax levied on non-Muslims by an Islamic state

Jummah: Friday prayer

K

Kaffir: a non-Muslim or infidel

Kitman: "to hide" or "to conceal"

Kufi: round beany type hate worn by Muslim men

L

M

Mecca: a city in Saudi Arabia that was the birthplace of Muhammad and is the holiest city of Islam

Medina: a city in western Saudi Arabia; site of the tomb of Muhammad; the second most holy city of Islam

Mujahideen: one engaged in jihad, fighters

N

P

PBUH: Peace Be Upon Him

Q

Quran: Muslims believe the Quran is a compilation of revelations given to the Prophet Muhammad by the angel Gabriel. The Quran is considered the Holy Book of Muslims.

R

S

Sharia: Archaic religious judicial system, which regulates the entire social life of Muslims and non-Muslims under Islamic dominance. Believed by Muslims to be God-given, it is immutable.

Shahada: Islamic profession of faith, "There is no god but Allah, and Muhammad is the Messenger of the Allah." The first pillar

Sunnah: verbally transmitted record of the teachings, deeds and sayings, silent permissions (or disapprovals) of the Islamic prophet Muhammad, as well as various reports about Muhammad's companions.

Sura: A chapter or portion of the Quran.

S.W.T. - SUBHANAHU WA TAA'LA

T

Tarbiyah - Training of a Da'ee in the art of Dawah

Tawhid: Oneness, unity

Tayiqqa: The art of deception, a form of religious dissimulation whereby a Muslim can deny his faith or commit otherwise illegal or blasphemous acts while they are at risk of significant persecution. It is explicitly supported by Qur'anic verses that instruct Muslims not to "take for friends or helpers Unbelievers rather than believers… except by way of precaution," and to not utter unbelief "except [while] under compulsion". Critics of Islam often conflate the doctrine of taqiyyah with that of lying in general, mislabeling all forms of lying as an example of "taqiyya".

Tazkiyah - Purification of life- thoughts and actions

U

Ummah: The collective worldwide body of Muslim believers.

V

W

X

Y

Z

Zakat: A charity tax, and one of the five pillars of Islam. The majority of Islamic scholars agree that non-Muslims should not benefit from this alms giving. One of the five pillars.

Groups

Muslim Brotherhood: Founded in Egypt in 1928 by Hassan al Banna. Their goal is to re-establish a global caliphate so that all people become Muslims and live according to Islamic law (sharia). Currently present in the United States as an umbrella under which 28 other organizations fall under, they believe infiltration from within is most effective. The Muslim Brotherhood is a designated terrorist organization across the Middle East, but not in the United States.

ISIS: The group has referred to itself as the Islamic State since it proclaimed a worldwide caliphate in June 2014 and named Abu Bakr al-Baghdadi as its caliph. As a caliphate, it claims religious, political and military authority over all Muslims worldwide. The goal of ISIS is to re-establish the global caliphate, particularly in the West, using violence as its means to accomplish this goal.

Hamas: Islamic Resistance Movement of a Palestinian Islamic organization, with an associated military wing. Located in Palestine, but operating in the United States, the goal is to liberate Palestine, including modern-day Israel, from Israeli occupation and to establish an Islamic state in the area that is now Israel, the West Bank and the Gaza Strip. Hamas is a designated terrorist organization by the United States State Dept.

NAIT: North American Islamic Trust: The North American Islamic Trust (NAIT) is a Saudi-backed organization based in Plainfield, Indiana, that owns Islamic properties and promotes waqf (Islamic endowments) in North America. It is the financial arm of the Muslim Students Association. NAIT finances and holds titles to mosques, Islamic schools, and other real estate.

CAIR: Council on American Islamic Relations formerly the Islamic Association of Palestine- claims to be the largest Muslim grassroots group in America. CAIR is an un-indicted co-conspirator in our nation's largest terrorism funding trial, The Holy Land Foundation, for monetarily supporting Hamas. Its Executive Director of the National chapter, Nihad Awad, is a self-proclaimed supporter of Hamas. CAIR is a designated Terrorist organization in the United Arab Emirates (U.A.E). CAIR has submitted arguments to a Texas District Court to have the label un-indicted co-conspirator removed, however the judge ruled there was substantial evidence to prove they did in fact fund Hamas.

CAIR has chapters in several states, and is famous for its lawsuits and demands for sensitivity training. CAIR has members in law enforcement, city councils, and federal agencies with several members serving in the White House.

MSA: The Muslim Student Association, with 600 chapters located on college campuses and universities in the United States and Canada, the Muslim Students Association (MSA) is the most visible and influential Islamic student organization in North America. Their purpose is to raise money and to perform Dawa, or to spread the word of Islam to bring non-Muslims to Islam.

USCMO: United States Council of Muslim Organizations. First proactive, Muslim Brotherhood political party. The formation of this coalition is significant as it has been legitimized by the current administration, and Congressmen Keith Ellison and Andre Carson.

The following document, which has been referred to through-out this book, is called **"An Explanatory Memorandum on the Strategic Goal for the Group in North America."** It is the play-book of the Muslim Brotherhood. It was placed into evidence during the Holy Land Foundation Trial in Dallas TX in 2008. They do not dispute or deny its existence, only we do.

EXPLANATORY MEMORANDUM

On the General Strategic Goal for the Group in North America
5/22/1991

In the name of God, the Beneficent, the Merciful Thanks be to God, Lord of the Two Worlds and Blessed are the Pious

The beloved brother/The General Masul, may God keep him
The beloved brother/Secretary of the Shura Council, may God keep him
The beloved brothers/Members of the Shura Council, may God keep them
God's peace, mercy and blessings be upon you.... To proceed,

I ask Almighty God that you, your families and those whom you love around you are in the best of conditions, pleasing to God, glorified His name be.

I send this letter of mine to you hoping that it would seize your attention and receive your good care as you are the people of responsibility and those to whom trust is given. Between your hands is an "Explanatory Memorandum" which I put effort in writing down so that it is not locked in the chest and the mind, and so that I can share with you a portion of the responsibility in leading the Group in this country.

What might have encouraged me to submit the memorandum in this time in particular is my feeling of a "glimpse of hope" and the beginning of good tidings which bring the good news that we have embarked on a new stage of Islamic activism stages in this continent. The papers which are between your hands are not abundant extravagance, imaginations or hallucinations which passed in the mind of one of your brothers, but they are rather hopes, ambitions and challenges that I hope that you share some or most of which with me. I do not claim their infallibility or absolute correctness, but they are an attempt which requires study, outlook, detailing and rooting from you.

My request to my brothers is to read the memorandum and to write what they wanted of comments and corrections, keeping in mind that what is between your hands is not strange or a new submission without a root, but rather an attempt to interpret and explain some of what came in the long-term plan which we approved and adopted in our council and our conference in the year (1987).

So, my honorable brother, do not rush to throw these papers away due to your many occupations and worries. All what I'm asking of you is to read them and to comment on them hoping that we might continue together the project of our plan and our Islamic work in this part of the world. Should you do that, I would be thankful and grateful to you.

I also ask my honorable brother, the Secretary of the Council, to add the subject of the memorandum on the Council agenda in its coming meeting.

May God reward you good and keep you for His Dawah

In the name of God, the Beneficent, the Merciful Thanks be to God, Lord of the Two Worlds and Blessed are the Pious

Subject: A project for an explanatory memorandum for the General Strategic goal for the Group in North America mentioned in the long-term plan

The Memorandum is derived from:

The general strategic goal of the Group in America which was approved by the Shura Council and the Organizational Conference for the year [1987] is "Enablement of Islam in North America, meaning: establishing an effective and a stable Islamic Movement led by the Muslim Brotherhood which adopts Muslims' causes domestically and globally, and which works to expand the observant Muslim base, aims at unifying and directing Muslims' efforts, presents Islam as a civilization alternative, and supports the global Islamic State wherever it is".

The priority that is approved by the Shura Council for the work of the Group in its current and former session which is "Settlement". The positive development with the brothers in the Islamic Circle in an attempt to reach a unity of merger. The constant need for thinking and future planning, an attempt to read it and working to "shape" the present to comply and suit the needs and challenges of the future. The paper of his eminence, the General Masul, may God keep him, which he recently sent to the members of the Council.

An Introduction to the Explanatory Memorandum:

In order to begin with the explanation, we must "summon" the following question and place it in front of our eyes as its relationship is important and necessary with the strategic goal and the explanation project we are embarking on. The question we are facing is: "How do you like to see the Islam Movement in North America in ten years?", or "taking along" the following sentence when planning and working, "Islamic Work in North America in the year (2000): A Strategic Vision".

Also, we must summon and take along "elements" of the general strategic goal of the Group in North America and I will intentionally repeat them in numbers. They are:

Establishing an effective and stable Islamic Movement led by the Muslim Brotherhood.

Adopting Muslims' causes domestically and globally.

Expanding the observant Muslim base.

Unifying and directing Muslims' efforts.

Presenting Islam as a civilization alternative

Supporting the establishment of the global Islamic State wherever it is

It must be stressed that it has become clear and emphatically known that all is in agreement that we must "settle" or "enable" Islam and its Movement in this part of the world.

Therefore, a joint understanding of the meaning of settlement or enablement must be adopted, through which and on whose basis we explain the general strategic goal with its six elements for the Group in North America.

The Concept of Settlement:

This term was mentioned in the Group's "dictionary" and documents with various meanings in spite of the fact that everyone meant one thing with it. We believe that the understanding of the essence is the same and we will attempt here to give the word and its "meanings" a practical explanation with a practical Movement tone, and not a philosophical linguistic explanation, while stressing that this explanation of ours is not complete until our explanation of "the process" of settlement itself is understood which is mentioned in the following paragraph. We briefly say the following:

Settlement: "That Islam and its Movement become a part of the homeland it lives in". Establishment: "That Islam turns into firmly-rooted organizations on whose bases civilization, structure and testimony are built". Stability: "That Islam is stable in the land on which its people move". Enablement: "That Islam is enabled within the souls, minds and the lives of the people of the country in which it moves". Rooting: "That Islam is resident and not a passing thing, or rooted "entrenched" in the soil of the spot where it moves and not a strange plant to it".

<u>The Process of Settlement:</u>
In order for Islam and its Movement to become "a part of the homeland" in which it lives, "stable" in its land, "rooted" in the spirits and minds of its people, "enabled" in the live of its society and has firmly-established "organizations" on which the Islamic structure is built and with which the testimony of civilization is achieved, the Movement must plan and struggle to obtain "the keys" and the tools of this process in carry out this grand mission as a "Civilization Jihadist" responsibility which lies on the shoulders of Muslims and - on top of them - the Muslim Brotherhood in this country. Among these keys and tools are the following:

Adopting the concept of settlement and understanding its practical meanings: The Explanatory Memorandum focused on the Movement and the realistic dimension of the process of settlement and its practical meanings without paying attention to the difference in understanding between the resident and the non-resident, or who is the settled and the non-settled and we believe that what was mentioned in the long-term plan in that regards suffices.

Making a fundamental shift in our thinking and mentality in order to suit the challenges of the settlement mission. What is meant with the shift - which is a positive expression - is responding to the grand challenges of the settlement issues. We believe that any transforming response begins with the method of thinking and its center, the brain, first. In order to clarify what is meant with the shift as a key to qualify us to enter the field of settlement, we say very briefly that the following must be accomplished:

A shift from the partial thinking mentality to the comprehensive thinking mentality.

A shift from the "amputated" partial thinking mentality to the "continuous" comprehensive mentality.

A shift from the mentality of caution and reservation to the mentality of risk and controlled liberation.

A shift from the mentality of the elite Movement to the mentality of the popular Movement.

A shift from the mentality of preaching and guidance to the mentality of building and testimony

A shift from the single opinion mentality to the multiple opinion mentality.

A shift from the collision mentality to the absorption mentality.

A shift from the individual mentality to the team mentality.

A shift from the anticipation mentality to the initiative mentality.

A shift from the hesitation mentality to the decisiveness mentality.

A shift from the principles mentality to the programs mentality.

A shift from the abstract ideas mentality the true organizations mentality [This is the core point and the essence of the memorandum].

Understanding the historical stages in which the Islamic Ikhwani activism went through in this country: The writer of the memorandum believes that understanding and comprehending the historical stages of the Islamic activism which was led and being led by the Muslim Brotherhood in this continent is a very important key in working towards settlement, through which the Group observes its march, the direction of its movement and the curves and turns of its road. We will suffice here with mentioning the title for each of these stages [The title expresses the prevalent characteristic of the stage] [Details maybe mentioned in another future study]. Most likely, the stages are:

The stage of searching for self and determining the identity. - The stage of inner build-up and tightening the organization. - The stage of mosques and the Islamic centers. - The stage of building the Islamic organizations - the first phase. - The stage of building the Islamic schools - the first phase. - The stage of thinking about the overt Islamic Movement - the first phase. - The stage of openness to the other Islamic movements and attempting to reach a formula for dealing with them - the first phase. - The stage of reviving and establishing the Islamic organizations - the second phase.

We believe that the Group is embarking on this stage in its second phase as it has to open the door and enter as it did the first time.

Understanding the role of the Muslim Brother in North America: The process of settlement is a "Civilization-Jihadist Process" with all the word means. The Ikhwan must understand that their work in America is a kind of grand Jihad in eliminating and destroying the Western civilization from within and "sabotaging" its miserable house by their hands and the hands of the believers so that it is eliminated and God's religion is made victorious over all other religions. Without this level of understanding, we are not up to this challenge and have not prepared ourselves for Jihad yet. It is a Muslim's destiny to perform Jihad and work wherever he is and wherever he lands until the final hour comes, and there is no escape from that destiny except for those who chose to slack. But, would the slackers and the Mujahedeen be equal.

Understanding that we cannot perform the settlement mission by ourselves or away from people: A mission as significant and as huge as the settlement mission needs magnificent and exhausting efforts. With their capabilities, human, financial and scientific resources, the Ikhwan will not be able to carry out this mission alone or away from people and he who believes that is wrong, and God knows best. As for the role of the Ikhwan, it is the initiative, pioneering, leadership, raising the banner and pushing people in that direction. They are then to work to employ, direct and unify Muslims' efforts and powers for this process. In order to do that, we must possess a mastery of the art of "coalitions", the art of "absorption" and the principles of "cooperation".

The necessity of achieving a union and balanced gradual merger between private work and public work:
We believe that what was written about this subject is many and is enough. But, it needs a time and a practical frame so that what is needed is achieved in a gradual and a balanced way that is compatible with the process of settlement.

The conviction that the success of the settlement of Islam and its Movement in this country is a success to the global Islamic Movement and a true support for the sought-after state, God willing:
There is a conviction - with which this memorandum disagrees - that our focus in attempting to settle Islam in this country will lead to negligence in our duty towards the global Islamic Movement in supporting its project to establish the state. We believe that the reply is in two segments: One - The success of the Movement in America in establishing an observant Islamic base with power and effectiveness will be the best support and aid to the global Movement project.

Bate #ISE-SW 1B10/ 0000419
And the second - is the global Movement has not succeeded yet in "distributing roles" to its branches, stating what is the needed

from them as one of the participants or contributors to the project to establish the global Islamic state. The day this happens, the children of the American Ikhwani branch will have far-reaching impact and positions that make the ancestors proud.

Absorbing Muslims and winning them with all of their factions and colors in America and Canada for the settlement project, and making it their cause, future and the basis of their Islamic life in this part of the world:

This issues requires from us to learn "the art of dealing with the others", as people are different and people in many colors. We need to adopt the principle which says, "Take from people... the best they have", their best specializations, experiences, arts, energies and abilities. By people here we mean those within or without the ranks of individuals and organizations. The policy of "taking" should be with what achieves the strategic goal and the settlement process. But the big challenge in front of us is: how to connect them all in "the orbit" of our plan and "the circle" of our Movement in order to achieve "the core" of our interest. To me, there is no choice for us other than alliance and mutual understanding of those who desire from our religion and those who agree from our belief in work. And the U.S. Islamic arena is full of those waiting...., the pioneers.

What matters is bringing people to the level of comprehension of the challenge that is facing us as Muslims in this country, conviction of our settlement project, and understanding the benefit of agreement, cooperation and alliance. At that time, if we ask for money, a lot of it would come, and if we ask for men, they would come in lines. What matters is that our plan is "the criterion and the balance" in our relationship with others.

Here, two points must be noted; the first one: we need to comprehend and understand the balance of the Islamic powers in the U.S. arena [and this might be the subject of a future study]. The second point: what we reached with the brothers in "ICNA" is considered a step in the right direction, the beginning of good and the first drop that requires growing and guidance.

Re-examining our organizational and administrative bodies, the type **of** leadership and the method **of** selecting it with what suits the challenges **of** the settlement mission: The memorandum will be silent about details regarding this item even though it is logical and there is a lot to be said about it.

Growing and developing **our** resources and capabilities, **our** financial and human resources with what suits the magnitude **of** the grand mission:

If we examined the human and the financial resources the Ikhwan alone own in this country, we and others would feel proud and glorious. And if we add to them the resources of our friends and allies, those who circle in our orbit and those waiting on our banner, we would realize that we are able to open the door to settlement and walk through it seeking to make Almighty God's word the highest.

Utilizing the scientific method in planning, thinking and preparation of studies needed for the process of settlement.

Yes, we need this method, and we need many studies which aid in this civilization Jihadist operation. We will mention some of them briefly: The history of the Islamic presence in America, the history of the Islamic Ikhwani presence in America, Islamic movements, organizations and organizations: analysis and criticism, the phenomenon of the Islamic centers and schools: challenges, needs and statistics, Islamic minorities, Muslim and Arab communities, and the U.S. society's view of Islam and Muslims... And many other studies which we can direct our brothers and allies to prepare, either through their academic studies or through their educational centers or organizational tasking. What is important is that we start.

Agreeing on a flexible, balanced and a clear "mechanism" to implement the process of settlement within a specific, gradual and balanced "time frame" that is in-line with the demands and challenges of the process of settlement.

Understanding the U.S. society from its different aspects an understanding that "qualifies" us to perform the mission of settling our Dawa' in its country "and growing it" on its land.

Adopting a written "jurisprudence" that includes legal and movement bases, principles, policies and interpretations which are suitable for the needs and challenges of the process of settlement.

Agreeing on "criteria" and balances to be a sort of "antennas" or "the watch tower" in order to make sure that all of our priorities, plans, programs, bodies, leadership, monies and activities march towards the process of the settlement.

Adopting a practical, flexible formula through which our central work complements our domestic work.

Understanding the role and the nature of work of "The Islamic Center" in every city with what achieves the goal of the process of settlement:

The center we seek is the one which constitutes the "axis" of our Movement, the "perimeter" of the circle of our work, our "balance center", the "base" for our rise and our "Dar al-Arqam" to educate us, prepare us and supply our battalions in addition to being the "niche" of our prayers.

This is in order for the Islamic center to turn - in action not in words - into a seed "for a small Islamic society" which is a reflection and a mirror to our central organizations. The center ought to turn into a "beehive" which produces sweet honey. Thus, the Islamic center would turn into a place for study, family, battalion, course, seminar, visit, sport, school, social club, women gathering, kindergarten for male and female youngsters, the office of the domestic political resolution, and the center for distributing our newspapers, magazines, books and our audio and visual tapes.

In brief we say: we would like for the Islamic center to become "The House of Dawa'" and "the general center" in deeds first before name. As much as we own and direct these centers at the continent level, we can say we are marching successfully towards the settlement of Dawa' in this country.

Meaning that the "center's" role should be the same as the "mosque's" role during the time of God's prophet, God's prayers and peace be upon him, when he marched to "settle" the Dawa' in its first generation in Madina. from the mosque, he drew the Islamic life and provided to the world the most magnificent and fabulous civilization humanity knew.

This mandates that, eventually, the region, the branch and the Usra turn into "operations rooms" for planning, direction, monitoring and leadership for the Islamic center in order to be a role model to be followed.

Adopting a system that is based on "selecting" workers, "role distribution" and "assigning" positions and responsibilities is based on specialization, desire and need with what achieves the process of settlement and contributes to its success.

Turning the principle of dedication for the Masuls of main positions within the Group into a rule, a basis and a policy in work. Without it, the process of settlement might be stalled [Talking about this point requires more details and discussion].

Understanding the importance of the "Organizational" shift in our Movement work, and doing Jihad in order to achieve it in the real world with what serves the process of settlement and expedites its results, God Almighty's willing:
The reason this paragraph was delayed is to stress its utmost importance as it constitutes the heart and the core of this memorandum. It also constitutes the practical aspect and the true measure

of our success or failure in our march towards settlement. The talk about the organizations and the "organizational" mentality or phenomenon does not require much details. It suffices to say that the first pioneer of this phenomenon was our prophet Mohamed, God's peace, mercy and blessings be upon him, as he placed the foundation for the first civilized organization which is the mosque, which truly became "the comprehensive organization". And this was done by the pioneer of the contemporary Islamic Dawa', Imam martyr Hasan al-Banna, may God have mercy on him, when he and his brothers felt the need to "re-establish" Islam and its movement anew, leading him to establish organizations with all their kinds: economic, social, media, scouting, professional and even the military ones. We must say that we are in a country which understands no language other than the language of the organizations, and one which does not respect or give weight to any group without effective, functional and strong organizations.

Bate #ISE-SW 1B10/ 0000422

It is good fortune that there are brothers among us who have this "trend", mentality or inclination to build the organizations who have beat us by action and words which leads us to dare say honestly what Sadat in Egypt once said, "We want to build a country of organizations" - a word of right he meant wrong with. I say to my brothers, let us raise the banner of truth to establish right "We want to establish the Group of organizations", as without it we will not able to put our feet on the true path.

And in order for the process of settlement to be completed, we must plan and work from now to equip and prepare ourselves, our brothers, our apparatuses, our sections and our committees in order to turn into comprehensive organizations in a gradual and balanced way that is suitable with the need and the reality. What encourages us to do that - in addition to the aforementioned -is that we possess "seeds" for each organization from the organization we call for.

All we need is to tweak them, coordinate their work, collect their elements and merge their efforts with others and then connect them with the comprehensive plan we seek. For instance, we have a seed for a "comprehensive media and art" organization, we own a print and advanced typesetting machine, an audio and visual center, art production office magazines in Arabic and English (The Horizons, The Hope, The Politicians, Ha Falastine, Press Clips, al-Zaytouna, Palestine Monitor, Social Sciences Magazines), art band, photographers, producers, programs anchors, journalists and in addition to other media and art experiences". Another example:

We have a seed for a "comprehensive Dawa educational" organization. We have the Dawa section in ISNA and Dr. Jamal Badawi Foundation, the center run by brother Hamed al-Ghazali and the Dawa center and Dawa Committee Brother Shaker al-Sayyed are seeking to establish now. In addition to other Dawa efforts here and there. And this applies to all the organizations we call on establishing.

The big challenge that is ahead of us is how to turn these seeds or "scattered" elements into comprehensive, stable, "settled" organizations that are connected with our Movement and which fly in our orbit and take orders from our guidance. This does not prevent - but calls for - each central organization to have its local branches but its connection with the Islamic center in the city is a must. What is needed is to seek to prepare the atmosphere and the means to achieve "the merger" so that the sections, the committees, the regions, the branches and the Usras are eventually the heart and the core of these organizations.

Comprehensive Settlement Organization: We would then seek and struggle in order to make each one of these above-mentioned organizations a "comprehensive organization" throughout the days and the years, and as long as we are destined to be in this country. What is important is that we put the foundation and we will be followed by peoples and generations that would finish the march and the road but with a clearly-defined guidance.

And, in order for us to clarify what we mean with the comprehensive, specialized organization, we mention here the characteristics and traits of each organization of the "promising" organizations.

From the Dawa' and educational aspect [The Dawa* and Educational Organization]: to include: The organization to spread the Dawa' (Central and local branches), an institute to graduate Callers and Educators, Scholars, Callers, Educators, Preachers and Program Anchors,

A television station, specialized Dawa' magazine, a radio station, the Higher Islamic Council for Callers and Educators, the Higher Council for Mosques and Islamic Centers and Friendship Societies with the other religions... and things like that.

Politically [The Political Organization]: to include: A central political party, local political offices, Political symbols, relationships and alliances, the American Organization for Islamic Political Action and Advanced Information Centers....and things like that.

Media [The Media and Art Organization]: to include: A daily newspaper, Weekly, monthly and seasonal magazines, radio stations, television programs, audio and visual centers, a magazine for the Muslim child, a magazine for the Muslim woman, print and typesetting machines, a production office, a photography and recording studio, art bands for acting, chanting and theater and a marketing and art production office... and things like that.

Economically [The Economic Organization: to include: An Islamic Central bank, Islamic endowments investment projects, and an organization for interest-free loans, and things like that.

Scientifically and Professionally [The Scientific. Educational and Professional Organization]: to include:_Scientific research centers, technical organizations and vocational training, an Islamic university, Islamic schools, a council for education and scientific research, centers to train teachers, scientific societies in schools, an office for academic guidance, and a body for authorship and Islamic curricula.... and things like that.

Culturally and Intellectually [The Cultural and Intellectual Organization]: to include: A center for studies and research, cultural and intellectual foundations such as [The Social Scientists Society - Scientists and Engineers Society, an organization for Islamic thought and culture, publication, translation and distribution house for Islamic books, an office for archiving, history and authentication, and a project to translate the Noble Quran, the Noble Sayings....and things like that.

Socially [The Social-Charitable Organization]: to include: Social clubs for the youths and the community's sons and daughters, local societies for social welfare and the services tied to the Islamic centers, the Islamic Organization to combat the social ills of the U.S. Society, Islamic houses project and matrimony and family cases office....and things like that.

(12)
Youths [The Youth Organization: to include: Central and local youth's foundations, sports teams and clubs and scouting teams.... and things like that.

Women [The Women Organization]: to include: Central and local women societies, organizations of training, vocational and housekeeping, an organization to train female preachers and Islamic kindergartens...and things like that.

Organizationally and Administratively [The Administrative and Organizational Organization: to include: An institute for training, growth, development and planning prominent experts in this field, work systems, bylaws and charters fit for running the most complicated bodies and organizations, a periodic magazine in Islamic development and administration, owning camps and halls for the various activities, a data, polling and census bank, an advanced communication network and an advanced archive for our heritage and production....and things like that.

Security [The Security Organization: to include: Clubs for training and learning self-defense techniques and a center which is concerned with the security issues [Technical, intellectual, technological and human] ....and things like that.

Legally [The Legal Organization]: to include: A Central Jurisprudence Council, a central Islamic Court, Muslim attorney's society, and The Islamic Foundation for Defense of Muslims' Rights...and things like that. And success is by God.

www.ingramcontent.com/pod-product-compliance
Lightning Source LLC
Chambersburg PA
CBHW072210280526

45788CB00002B/957